CAMBRIDGE LIBRARY COLLECTION

Books of enduring scholarly value

Women's Writing

The later twentieth century saw a huge wave of academic interest in women's writing, which led to the rediscovery of neglected works from a wide range of genres, periods and languages. Many books that were immensely popular and influential in their own day are now studied again, both for their own sake and for what they reveal about the social, political and cultural conditions of their time. A pioneering resource in this area is Orlando: Women's Writing in the British Isles from the Beginnings to the Present (http://orlando.cambridge.org), which provides entries on authors' lives and writing careers, contextual material, timelines, sets of internal links, and bibliographies. Its editors have made a major contribution to the selection of the works reissued in this series within the Cambridge Library Collection, which focuses on non-fiction publications by women on a wide range of subjects from astronomy to biography, music to political economy, and education to prison reform.

My Long Life

Mary Cowden Clarke (1809–98) was the daughter of the music publisher Vincent Novello. Charles and Mary Lamb were family friends, and under the inspiration of their *Tales from Shakespeare*, Mary became a noted Shakespeare scholar, her major work being the *Concordance to Shakespeare*, which took twelve years to compile, and was to remain a standard work for half a century. From 1856 Clarke and her husband Charles lived in Italy, continuing to publish essays and books, including their joint *Cassell's Illustrated Shakespeare*. This autobiography, published in 1896, contains many anecdotes and memories of the literary and musical circles in which Mary moved throughout her life: the Lambs, John Keats, the Shelleys, Dickens, Leigh Hunt and Mendelssohn all appear. The book is written in a vivid and engaging style, and records a fascinating nineteenth century life. For more information on this author, see http://orlando.cambridge.org/public/svPeople?person_id=clarmc

T0370794

Cambridge University Press has long been a pioneer in the reissuing of out-of-print titles from its own backlist, producing digital reprints of books that are still sought after by scholars and students but could not be reprinted economically using traditional technology. The Cambridge Library Collection extends this activity to a wider range of books which are still of importance to researchers and professionals, either for the source material they contain, or as landmarks in the history of their academic discipline.

Drawing from the world-renowned collections in the Cambridge University Library, and guided by the advice of experts in each subject area, Cambridge University Press is using state-of-the-art scanning machines in its own Printing House to capture the content of each book selected for inclusion. The files are processed to give a consistently clear, crisp image, and the books finished to the high quality standard for which the Press is recognised around the world. The latest print-on-demand technology ensures that the books will remain available indefinitely, and that orders for single or multiple copies can quickly be supplied.

The Cambridge Library Collection will bring back to life books of enduring scholarly value (including out-of-copyright works originally issued by other publishers) across a wide range of disciplines in the humanities and social sciences and in science and technology.

My Long Life

An Autobiographic Sketch

MARY COWDEN CLARKE

CAMBRIDGE UNIVERSITY PRESS

Cambridge, New York, Melbourne, Madrid, Cape Town, Singapore,
São Paolo, Delhi, Dubai, Tokyo, Mexico City

Published in the United States of America by Cambridge University Press, New York

www.cambridge.org
Information on this title: www.cambridge.org/9781108021975

This edition first published 1896
This digitally printed version 2010

ISBN 978-1-108-02197-5 Paperback

MY LONG LIFE

W.L.Colls.Ph Sc.

Mary Cowden: Clarke

MY LONG LIFE

An Autobiographic Sketch

By Mary Cowden-Clarke

Author of

'*The Concordance to Shakespeare*,'
'*The Girlhood of Shakespeare's Heroines*,'
'*The Iron Cousin*,' *Etc.*, *Etc.*

'I count myself in nothing else so happy,
As in a soul remembering my good friends.'
SHAKESPEARE.

Second Edition

LONDON
T. FISHER UNWIN
MDCCCXCVI.

LIST OF ILLUSTRATIONS

MY LONG LIFE

Having been asked to write my reminis-
cences of myself and of my family, and of
the persons distinguished in literature or
art whom I have known, I have the rather
consented because I have been blessed with
a greatly privileged and happy life.

I was born on the 22d of June 1809, in
the same house where my father, Vincent
Novello, was born—No. 240 Oxford Street,
or, as it was then called, Oxford *Road*, for
it still bore some traces of a somewhat
suburban exit from that western quarter of
London. Its vicinity to Hyde Park and
Kensington Gardens, its closeness to Edge-
ware Road and Bayswater Road, its commanding from its attic storey a distant
view of the Surrey Hills, combined to pro-

duce a rural as well as urban effect to the
impression upon my earliest days.   I used
to watch the waggon that jogged past our
door of an evening, with its tarpaulin cover
and its lantern swinging at its rear, and
thinking how delightful it would be to take
a journey into the country lolling inside this
comfortable conveyance.   The early market-
carts that rumbled by of a morning, with
their supply of fresh vegetables and fruit,
bringing a delicious air from the region of
meadows full of buttercups and daisies, made
me long to be out among the lanes and fields
these carts came from.   But even Hyde Park,
where I was entrusted to convoy my younger
brothers and sisters, supplied me with enjoyment of those fine old elm trees, those
stretches of grass I beheld.   Such things as
halfpenny little mugs of curds and whey
were extant in those days—sold near to the
Park entrance, then called Cumberland Gate,
now known as the Marble Arch ; and which
dainty refection seemed properly rustic and
appropriate.   The railing adjacent to the

gate was, at that period, permitted to be strung with rows of printed old-fashioned ballads, such as ‘Cruel Barbara Allen,’ etc.

To give an idea of the then neighbourhood, there was a small stationery shop in Quebec Street, kept by a Miss Lavoine, where we children bought slates and slate-pencils ; and a certain bakery in Bryanston Street that had a curved iron railing below its shop window, which tempted us to spend some of our pocket money in pennyworths of old-world gingerbread figure-cakes, in the shape of lions, tigers, horses, dogs, cocks and hens, castles, alphabets and other objects, besides selling crisp squares of ‘parliament,’ crunched by us with considerable satisfaction. A few doors farther down Oxford Street there was a grocer’s shop kept by a Mr Harvey, whose snow-white hair and jet-black eyes remain pictured in my memory, and who used, when my mother bought tea and sugar of him, to make up a small packet of the caraway comfits that occupied one of his shop windows, together with heart-shaped hoarhound, etc., presenting the aforesaid packet to us. We must have been conscientiously brought-up little people; for once, when a young man I had never seen before was standing behind the counter in lieu of the master, and was proceeding to make up the usual packet, I said to him : 'Did Mr Harvey allow you to give us those sugar-plums?' He smiled and replied : 'I am doing this for him. I am Mr Harvey's son.' I may mention here another instance of our conscientious bring-ing-up.

I went to a party of young people, where they were playing at a round game of cards, and they asked me to join them. When the nursery-maid came to fetch me home, the lady of the house offered me some silver, saying : 'Take this seven-and-sixpence, you have won it.' 'I thought,' I replied, 'that we were playing with counters; I saw them on the table, ma'am. I did not know we were playing for money. I have none, and could not have paid if I had lost. Therefore I can't have won, and can't take that silver.' When I went home and told my mother what had happened, she said : 'You did well to refuse the money, and gave the right reason for doing so.'

One of the children's parties we were invited to every year was given on the Feast of the Holy Innocents by an old French gentleman and his sister, Mr and Miss Lamour. He was very kind to children, though so notoriously irate at whist that we recognised him many years after at Nice by the description a gentleman gave of him as the man who most lost his temper at whist ever known. But on those old-time parties of the Holy Innocents' evening, Mr Lamour used to play the violin for us while we danced, and encouraged us to sing after helping round high piles of muffins and crumpets, and finally sending each little child home with a packet of cakes, and almonds and raisins.

Another of our urban delights in those days was watching, from the window of our front-parlour nursery, 'the soldiers' as they passed by from the barracks in Portman Street to parade in Hyde Park. First came a magnificent and imperious drum-major, who, notwithstanding the importance with which he wielded his tall staff of office, seeming solemnly to pick his way with it, used to cast a smiling eye toward the group of young faces that peered admiringly over the low, green blind at him and his brilliant troop preceded by its band of music.

One of the chief figures among these was a black man, who brandished and clashed a pair of dazzling cymbals ; and another was also a black, who upheld a kind of oriental standard that had horse tails dangling therefrom, and jingling bells pendant from a central silver crescent.

I do not know whether these figures still form part of the British military band, but they impressively dazzle and give picturesqueness to my memory of it in that epoch. They add brilliancy to those mornings, and strengthen the contrast they afford with the dimness of the previous evenings, for Oxford

Street was then lighted at night by oil lamps, gas lighting not being invented.

Opposite to our house was Camelford House, where Prince Leopold and Princess Charlotte resided when in town, and a pleasant sight it used to be to me to watch the Prince with the Princess beside him—he driving his curricle, with its glittering steel bar across the prancing horses, and the out-riders in their green and gold Coburg livery —setting forth to take an airing round Hyde Park. Once I saw her going to Court, the indispensable hoop tilted sideways to enable her to take her seat in the carriage, and the equally indispensable huge plume of feathers then required for Court costume. When her early death threw all England into mourn-ing—for no one, however poor, but had at least a scrap of crape about them—my father set to music Leigh Hunt's touching verses, —'His departed love to Prince Leopold.'

My two brothers, Alfred and Edward, when quite little boys, were sent to a Mr Foothead's preparatory school in the New

Road, and I used to escort them there, we three trundling our hoops along Baker Street, after stopping to peep through the railings round the gardens of Montague House and think of the legend about Mrs Montague's finding her son (whom she had lost when straying in the streets) in the person of a little sooty climbing boy, who had been stolen by a master chimney-sweep, had been unwittingly sent to the very house where he was born, that he might sweep its chimneys, but had, by some subtlety of instinctive sympathy, crept into one of its beds and was found there by his own mother.

Our parents were bountiful in providing us with books ; plain, unornate books—very unlike the present juvenile volumes, full of highly-coloured illustrations, often scarcely read by their young recipients, so lavishly are these gifts bestowed by fond relations and friends—but fewer in number, and diligently perused over and over again, reread and treasured by us young Novellos. First, there was Mrs Barbauld's ' Charles-

Book ' (as we used to call it) ; then came Miss Edgeworth's ' Frank,' ' Rosamond ' and ' Parents' Assistant ' ; Day's ' Sandford and Merton ' ; the wise and cheerful ' Evenings at Home' ; ' A Visit for a Week ' ; ' The Juvenile Travellers ' ; ' The 100 Wonders of the World' ; ' The Book of Trades ' and 'Æsop's Fables.' Often, after a hard day's teaching, my father used to have his breakfast in bed next morning, when we children were allowed to scramble up to the counterpane and lie around him to see what new book he had bought for us, and listen to his description and explanation of it. Never can I forget the boundless joy and interest with which I heard him tell about the contents of two volumes he had just brought home, and showed me the printed pictures it had. It was an early edition of ' Lamb's Tales from Shakespeare.' And what a vast world of new ideas and new delights that opened to me—a world in which I have ever since much dwelt, and always with supreme pleasure and admiration.

On Sundays I knelt beside my mother in
the Portuguese Embassy's Chapel, South
Street, Grosvenor Square, where my father
was organist for six-and-twenty years. A
central figure in the picture that small
sanctuary has painted on my memory is that
of my godfather, the Reverend William Victor
Fryer, as he officiated at the altar, irradiated
by the light from the tall wax candles thereon, and when he stood in the pulpit de-
livering the sermon. His attitude here was
simple yet impressive, and it is the attitude
represented in the pencil portrait of him,
drawn by Wageman, who was famous for
his correct likenesses. I have that portrait
still, and it shows Mr Fryer standing with
raised hand, holding a cambric pocket-hand-
kerchief, his most usual position while preaching. It was from the Reverend William
Victor Fryer that I obtained my second name,
Victoria ; and from my mother my first
name, Mary. To him my father dedicated
his first work, ' Sacred Music,' in two vols. ;
and this, with several Masses composed by

himself, besides introducing Mozart's and Haydn's Masses for the first time in England, were performed at South Street chapel by my father. His organ-playing attained such renown that it attracted numerous persons, even among the nobility, whose carriages waited for them outside while they lingered to the end of the service, and after; for it was playfully said that his ' voluntaries '— intended to ' play out ' the congregation—on the contrary, kept them in, listening to the very last note.

The evening parties at 240 Oxford Street were marked by a judicious economy blended with the utmost refinement and good taste ; the supper refection was of the simplest— Elia's ' Chapter on Ears ' eloquently recording the ' friendly supper-tray ' and draught of ' true Lutheran Beer ' which succeeded to the feasts of music provided by the host's playing on the small but fine-toned chamber organ, which occupied one end of the graceful drawing-room. This was papered with a delicately-tinted pink colour, showing to advantage the choice water-colour paintings by Varley, Copley Fielding, Havell and Cristall that hung around. These artists were all personally known to Vincent Novello, and were not unfrequent visitors on these occasions. The floor was covered by a plain grey drugget, bordered by a beautiful garland of grapes and vine-leaves, designed and worked by my mother herself. Besides the guests above named, there were often present Charles and Mary Lamb, Leigh Hunt, John Keats and ever-welcome, ever young-hearted Charles Cowden-Clarke. My enthusiasm—child as I was—for these distinguished visitors was curiously strong. I can remember once creeping round to where Leigh Hunt's hand rested on the back of the sofa upon which he sat, and giving it a quiet kiss—because I heard he was *a poet*. And I have even now full recollection of the reverent look with which I regarded John Keats, as he leaned against the side of the organ, listening with rapt attention to my father's music. Keats's favourite position

—one foot raised on his other knee—still remains imprinted on my memory ; as also does the last time I saw him, half-reclining on some chairs that formed a couch for him when he was staying at Leigh Hunt's house, just before leaving England for Italy. Another poet reminiscence I have—of jumping up to peer over the parlour window-blind to have a peep at Shelley, who I had heard was leaving, after a visit he had just paid to my father upstairs. Well was I rewarded, for, as he passed before our house, he gave a glance up at it, and I beheld his seraph-like face, with its blue eyes, and aureoled by its golden hair.

An enchanting treat of those childish years was what we called 'a day in the fields.' Our place of assembling was generally some spot between Hampstead and Highgate (no Regent's Park or Zoological Gardens then in existence !) and there we met, by appointment, Leigh Hunt and his family, the Gliddons and their families, our company being often enhanced in brightness by the advent from town of lively Henry Robertson and ever-young Charles Cowden-Clarke. The picnic part of our entertainment was cold lamb and salad prepared by my mother, she being an acknowledged adept in the dressing of this latter. Other toothsome cates supplemented the out-of-door dinner, while more intellectual food was not wanting. Leigh Hunt once read out to us Dogberry's 'Charge to the Watchmen,' and another time gave us the two scenes, from Sheridan's 'Rivals,' between Sir Anthony and his son. Leigh Hunt's reading aloud was the perfection of spirited perusal. He possessed innate fascination of voice, look and manner. While he was in Horsemonger Lane Jail for the libel on the Prince Regent, Mr John Clarke, master of the school at Enfield, in accordance with his son Charles's wish, used to send by him fresh vegetables and fruit to Leigh Hunt from the Enfield garden. This was the school where John Keats was educated, and where he learned to love poetry from his 'Friend Charles,' as he styles him in his noble 'Epistle to Charles Cowden-Clarke.'

When Leigh Hunt left prison, my father asked him to sit for his portrait to Wageman—a dearly-prized portrait that I still have near me in my own room. It is the very best likeness I have ever seen of him; and well do I remember his poet face and his bent head, with its jet-black hair, as he wrote his name beneath the pencil drawing.

During our childhood we had some healthful changes to other air than that of London. On one occasion my parents took us, by one of the earliest steam-vessels that plied on the Thames (called a Margate Hoy), for a short trip to the seaside. As this steamer left the London Docks, I heard a man in a wherry bawl out jeeringly,—'I say! bile up yere kettle!' We had made some way down the river when a portion of the machinery broke, and there was much confusion and alarm on deck among the passengers. My dear mother bade me hide my head in her lap and remain still. I did so, and she praised me for my quiet and obedience. The vessel managed to reach the shore; we disembarked; and I remember my father carrying the then baby in his arms while we all walked across the fields towards Milton or Settingbourne, at one of which places, on the Kentish High Road, we had to stay till next day, when we could proceed on our journey by the stage-coach. We were still young children when our parents removed from 240 Oxford Street to 8 Percy Street, Bedford Square; and soon after our removal thither, my mother resolved to take us to Boulogne - sur - Mer for a thorough 'sea change,' and in order that we might gain some idea of French and French environments. We travelled by the stage-coach to Dover (there were no railways then), but when we arrived there, it was found that the wind did not serve for the sailing-packet to cross the Channel, so we had to stay for three days at an inn,

ÆT. 53
1834

VINCENT NOVELLO.

till we could embark. When we reached
our destination, we boarded in the house
of a very stout, good-natured woman, with
numerous stalwart sons — fishermen, all.
Halfway up the Grande Rue, leading from
the lower town to the high town, there
was a school kept by a Mr Bonnefoy, who
had a comfortable, motherly woman for a
wife; and she not only brought up well
her own children, but took kindly care of
the schoolboys. Here my mother decided
to leave my eldest brother, Alfred, for a
twelvemonth, that he might learn to speak
the language; and so thoroughly was this
accomplished, that he spoke it fluently, and
even, he said, began to *think* in French,
thus familiar had it become. When we
other children returned home, dear, kind
Mary Lamb offered to give me lessons
in Latin, and to teach me to read verse
properly—an offer eagerly accepted for me
by my father and mother. I used, therefore, to trudge regularly, on appointed
mornings, to Great Russell Street, Covent

Garden, where the Lambs then lived ; and one morning, when I entered the room, I saw a lady sitting with Miss Lamb, whom I heard say,—'Oh, I am now nothing but a stocking - mending old woman.' This lady had straight, black brows, and looked still young, I thought, and had a very intelligent, expressive countenance. When she went away, Miss Lamb said,—'That is the excellent actress, Miss Kelly. Look at her well, Victoria, for she is a woman to remember having seen.' And, indeed, this was no other than the admirable artist to whom Charles Lamb addressed his two sonnets ; the one beginning,—

'You are not, Kelly, of the common strain,'

and the other, on her performance of 'The Blind Boy,' beginning,—

'Rare artist, who with half thy tools or none
  Canst execute with ease thy curious art.'

On a subsequent morning, a boy came rushing into the room and dashed through

the repetition of his Latin lesson with a
rapidity that dazzled me, and fired me with
ambition to repeat my conjugations in the
same brilliant style. When the boy was
gone—it was Hazlitt's son, whom Mary
Lamb also taught his Latin grammar—I
began trying to scamper through my lesson,
but Mary Lamb wisely stopped me, and
advised me not to attempt what was not in
my sober, steady way. She said, ' It is
natural to him, but not to you. Best be
natural in all you do, and in all you attempt.' Her reading poetry was beautifully
natural and unaffected ; so that her mode of
beginning Milton's 'Paradise Lost' for me
still remains on my mind's ear. In curious
contrast with Mary Lamb's lessons were
some that were given, once upon a time,
when a certain old Scotch gentleman was
engaged to teach Latin and arithmetic to
my brothers, Alfred and Edward, I being
allowed to share in the instruction received
from him. This Mr Ferguson was a
placidly pedantic person, and when the

servant-maid knelt down near him to lay the fire ready for lighting, he leaned down and told her how she could best place the coals 'so that the sulphureous particles should soonest ignite.'

A very pleasant incident was enjoyed by me in a few weeks' sojourn I had at a farmhouse near Tunbridge, whither my parents sent me, they knowing the worthy people whose farm it was. Delightful were those early mornings when I was despatched to another farm, about half-a-mile off, that I might drink new milk from the cow, after a walk through green lanes before breakfast. In those matutinal walks I was invariably accompanied by a kitten, who had taken a fancy to me, or who, perhaps, knew that she was to have a saucer of milk given to her when we arrived. I remember one morning a man on horseback stopped his steed to look with an amused laugh at a little girl followed by a kitten, like a dog, along a lane, the two quite alone in that quiet spot. Nutting and blackberrying for hours of an afternoon were delights to me ; and fetching up the ducks before night- fall was a grand privilege allotted to me. Glorious were those baking-days, when feasts of new-made bread, a Kentish delicacy called huffkins—a sort of muffin plentifully buttered and eaten hot—and a superb pork pie—con- taining alternate layers of potato, sage, and dairy-fed pork—formed the delicious peri- odically-appointed cates. But above all other joys to me was the finding, in an out-of- the-way corner of the farmhouse, an old edition of 'Sir Charles Grandison.' The book was printed in double columns, and had pictures in it. One which particularly interested me was that where Sir Hargrave Pollixfen is carrying off Miss Byron after the masquerade, bearing her forcibly into a chariot, meaning to marry her against her will. Ever after that first introduction to the story, the book, when I became allowed to read it, remained a favourite with me, and I have often been conscious of wishing that its many volumes were as many more.

From Percy Street my parents removed to
an old-fashioned house and garden on Shacklewell Green ; and my two elder brothers were
sent to Mr Yule's academy, near at hand.
Here my brother Alfred's familiarity with
French stood him in good stead, for he not
only translated with ease and correctness the
page of ' Recueil Choisi ' assigned to him and
to his schoolfellows as their daily task ; but
' the boys ' used to get possession of ' Novello's
slate ' and copy out his translation as their
own.

It was while we lived at Shacklewell that
my father and mother received letters from
Leigh Hunt (who was then in Italy), introducing the widowed Mrs Shelley and Mrs
Williams, who were returning to England
after their terrible bereavement.   He described Mrs Wollstonecraft's daughter as
' inclining, like a wise and kind being, to
receive all the consolation which the good
and kind can give her ; ' adding, ' she is as
quiet as a mouse, and will drink in as much
Mozart and Paesiello as you choose to afford

her.' Accordingly, many were the occasions when delicious hours of music and quiet, but animated and interesting, talk were planned for the two beautiful young women able and willing to enjoy such 'delights,' and choosing not unwisely 'to interpose them oft.' To meet thus were frequently invited my uncle, Francis Novello, who had a charming bass voice (he was the bass singer at South Street Chapel during the period when his brother Vincent was organist there) ; Henry Robertson, as excellent a tenor singer as he was excellent in lively companionship ; my father's pupil, Edward Holmes, a sterling musician and admirable judge of literature, moreover, a great admirer of the two lady guests, and Charles Cowden-Clarke, who shared in all these attainments and predilections with his never-failing, youthful enthusiasm. Mornings and afternoons witnessed numerous 'goings through' of Mozart's 'Cosi fan tutte,' 'Don Giovanni,' 'Nozze di Figaro' and various songs of Paesiello, besides other choice compositions by other composers ; and not a few evenings were spent by these well-pleased associates in prolonged discourse on attractive topics, till—forgetful of the lapse of time—the ladies declared they 'must go,' and were accompanied back to town by our gentlemen guests, only too pleased to be their escort. It was at this period that Mrs Shelley wrote my name on a copy of her ' Frankenstein ' which I had already devoured when given to me by my father, but which I ardently desired should have the glory of her name and mine together on its blank page. My father was her declared adorer, and she his, while Edward Holmes was equally unreserved in his bewitchment of her ; and they both united in attributing to Charles Cowden-Clarke a decided enthralment by the graces of Mrs Williams. Playful and mutual gaiety was the result ; while my dear mother joined in the jest — even her husband's and Mrs Shelley's avowed interchange of fascination. The Italian form of name evidently lingered musically in Mrs Shelley's ear, for she in-

variably addressed my father as 'Vincenzo,'
and his brother as 'Francesco.' She gave
my father a tress of her mother's hair, knowing that he had always had a great admiration
for Mary Wollstonecraft, although without
being personally acquainted with her. This
tress Mary Shelley accompanied by an affectionate little note to my father, in Italian,
which tress and note are still in my possession, carefully preserved under glass, and
treasured, among other relics of the kind, in
a collection of hair I have.

We were still residents at Shacklewell
Green, when my parents resolved to send me
for a time to Boulogne-sur-Mer, that I might
acquire the French language ; and they con-
fided me to the care of the friendly and
estimable Bonnefoy family. Old Monsieur
Bonnefoy was one of the most excellent of
tutors, and certainly one of the most simple-
minded of men. The naive way in which
he allowed himself to be supposed utterly
unaware of the preparations for a due celebration of his birthday (which was kept,

according to continental custom, on his namesake Saint's day, the feast of *St Pierre*) was quite remarkable. 'The boys' were allowed to go into the fields and gather armfuls of *Marguerites* without Monsieur Bonnefoy noticing that his scholars did not come to school at the usual hour ; his entering the schoolroom with complete ignorance of the boy mounted on a chair behind the door, ready to drop a daisy crown on his master's head, and wholly unprepared for the shout of applause that was to burst from the assembled concourse of scholars when the coronation feat was accomplished, formed a triumph of utter unconsciousness. He had, on ordinary occasions, what he considered an ingenious contrivance for obtaining attention when he addressed the boys, by twitching a string, attached to a ball, that lifted a moveable cover, beneath which appeared the word '*Silence!*' ; and though I believe it rarely obtained the desired object more effectually than a similar sound of bell-jangling per-

formed in the French House of Parliament (which I once witnessed when in Paris),
yet Monsieur Bonnefoy seemed perfectly
satisfied with the effect he produced in his
schoolroom. It was between the morning
and afternoon hours of school that my
kind old master gave me his daily lesson
in French, and very pleasant he made these
lessons, giving me 'dictation' from small
entertaining anecdotes and short stories,
contained in a book he chose for the purpose, besides imparting the drier instruction of grammar, spelling, etc., etc. My
parents had thoughtfully taken a season
ticket of admission to the theatre for Monsieur Bonnefoy and for me, as one of the
very best means of my gaining familiarity
with colloquial French ; so my old master
and I used to trudge together, very willingly, to the playhouse whenever there was
performance there. Thus I had the advantage of an introduction to Beaumarchais'
' Mariage de Figaro,' and to some of Molière's
fine comedies, besides other lighter and

shorter dramatic pieces. There was an actor
of the name of Duhez, who played admirably the part of Alceste in Molière's 'Misan-
thrope,' and whose look and manner still
remain visible to my memory, while the
recollection of such amusing trifles as '*Mes
derniers vingt sous*,' '*Le plus beau jour de
ma vie*,' etc., etc., leave the impression of
several agreeably-spent evenings. On those
evenings when the theatre was not open,
Monsieur Bonnefoy generally took me a
walk up to the high town, and we had
pleasant strolls round the ramparts there,
which commanded fine views and pure air,
and where he used to talk incessantly, telling me much of the time of his juvenile
days, when there was talk of an intended
invasion of England by Napoleon Buona-
parte, and when he, young Bonnefoy, served
for a time on board one of the frigates
then lying off Boulogne, and of his own
skill in navigation, acquired even in that
brief service. He was naively proud of
his knowledge, whatever its kind, and as

naively expressed his pride thereon. On one occasion, when my father's pupil, Edward Holmes, paid me a visit at Boulogne, on his way to Paris, I remember Monsieur Bonnefoy's indulging in openly-shown, amused scorn at the Englishman's astronomical ignorance by looking for the rising moon in the wrong quarter of the heavens. From our walks round the ramparts of the high town, we passed by a certain bookseller's shop, kept by a friend of Monsieur Bonnefoy's ; and he never failed to stop and have a chat with this friend, who was a lively, laughing man, and who used to show us any new works that he had added to his store. My days at Boulogne were passed most pleasantly and profitably as regarded my parents' views in sending me there. My health was strengthened, and my appetite was more vigorous than I have ever experienced it elsewhere. Early every morning I accompanied Madame Bonnefoy to the market-place, which occupied a broad space in

front of the *Cathédrale*. It formed a
brilliant and animated scene—the peasant
women with their many-coloured costumes,
the fishwomen with their baskets slung at
their backs, their high white caps, long gold
earrings (some mere dangling pendants,
others formed like acorns), their short petti-
coats and wooden shoes—all these people
chattering and screaming in broad *patois*
at the very top of their voices. Amidst
them Madame Bonnefoy good-humouredly
made her way, steadily making her purchases
for the day's consumption, piling them
into a large basket, carried by one of the
ever-ready *jeunes filles*, at hand for that
purpose. Eggs bought by the quarter-
hundred at a time, butter in gigantic pats
of the size and shape of a pine‑apple,
fresh vegetables and meat for the *pot-au-
feu*, set on to seethe and stew as soon as
we went back to the house. Madame
Bonnefoy was a super‑excellent cook, and
she devoted her culinary skill to the well-
being of her household. At stated periods

she made enormous loaves of *pain de ménage*, huge slices of which, buttered with unsparing hand, I used to dispose of with marvellous gusto. During the forenoon I studied my lessons ready for my mid-day tuition from Monsieur Bonnefoy ; and in the evening came the theatre, or the walk and talk on the ramparts with him.

On my return to England, it was agreed that I should begin my intended profession— that of a governess ; and an engagement was soon found for me in the family of a gentle- man and lady named Purcell, four of whose children I was to teach. The 'four' proved really to be five, for the youngest was oftener sent to the schoolroom than kept in the nursery. However, nothing could be kinder to me than the lady of the house. I was taken down, late one evening, in their chariot to their country residence at Cranford, and it was a curious experience to find myself seated in the dark, with perfect strangers beside me, and being driven to a spot I had never seen. But when I saw it next morning I found it a most attractive 'cottage orné.' Its ground-floor rooms were fitted up in the tastefullest style, one with a trellised papering of honey-suckles, interspersed with mirrors let into the wall ; another with roses, chandeliers, giran-doles, and so on, that took my girlish fancy immensely. Before seeing this pretty in-terior I had been into the garden, for I was always an early riser ; and, moreover, I wanted a quiet hour to make myself acquainted with my new surroundings, and also to look over the lessons I should have to give my young pupils during the day. Even thus immedi-ately I experienced the kindness of my lady-employer ; for when she learned that I had asked whether I might eat an apple that I found fallen on the grass, she gave me leave to take an apple from the tree whenever I felt inclined to eat one before breakfast. So young was I, that I was no more than two years older than my eldest pupil, and I soon became popular with her and her brothers when they found that, after lessons were over, I used to tell them stories, and even made a

small theatre for them, with books stuck up
for side-scenes, and paper dolls for the actors
and actresses. One of these paper performers
became so great a favourite with the children
that they called her 'Norah' (she generally
represented some faithful nurse or equally
estimable character), and invariably gave her
a round of applause when she made her appearance. The fame of these theatrical entertainments reaching the ears of the children's
mamma, she condescended to be present at
one of them, and gave her hearty approval.
One of my chief anxieties while I was a
governess was lest my pianoforte teaching
and playing should not fulfil the expectation
of my employers ; for whenever I was requested to come up to the drawing-room and
play a duet with either of my pupils, the
second one always executed her part with
unusual carelessness, infinitely less well than
she played at other times. I remember
especially one evening when I suffered an
agony of nervousness while playing with
Miss Celia an arrangement for four hands

of the fine overture to Weber's 'Freischütz' (which overture, by-the-bye, had the un-precedented compliment of being invariably encored at the theatre this first season of the opera's being brought out in London), for we both played so miserably that I pictured to myself the company in the drawing-room saying, 'Can this be Vincent Novello's daughter?' On the approach of winter, the family returned to town and occupied their house in Montague Square. This was a great pleasure to me, for I was nearer home and I could have news of my dear ones often. My father and mother indulged me with frequent letters, though at that time the post-age of a letter from even so near a place as Shacklewell to London was actually three-pence! But what treasures of parental tender-ness and fond encouragement those letters were. One of them from my father and one from my mother I have still, I'm grateful to say. These letters used to be brought into the schoolroom for me by Joe, a black servant, who had been a devotedly-attached attendant

upon Mrs Purcell when she was a young
child in the West Indies, and she had brought
him with her to Europe, where she retained
him in her service as footman. He was an
excellent fellow, sweet-natured and kindly.
When he entered the schoolroom with a
letter in his hand, his white teeth would
gleam through his grinning lips, his eyes
would sparkle with gladness, knowing that
he brought me happiness in this missive from
my parents. It was Joe whom his mistress
sent to attend me, when she wished that I
should go to the evening services of Com-
pline and Tenebræ at South Street Chapel,
as well as accompanying the children to
Mass and Vespers there; and I remember
how odd it seemed to me to be followed
in the street by a footman.

But besides my letters from home came
another great and unexpected joy to me, in
the shape of visits now and then from ever-
cheerful-spirited Charles Cowden-Clarke, who
lent me books and brought me direct news
from my parents. So bright, so genial, so

inspiriting was his presence, that he seemed
as though he had seen but scarce two decades
of existence, though in reality he had fully
entered upon his third.   Well might he thank
the Divine Giver 'for youth and mirth and
health' as he had done that very year before,
when he wrote his beautifully devout

HYMN TO GOD.

In Thy large temple—the blue depth of space—
And on the altar of Thy quiet fields,
(Fit shrine to hold the beauty of Thy love)
Great Spirit ! with earnest cheerfulness I place
This off'ring, which a grateful heart now yields,
For all those high and gracious thoughts that rove
O'er all Thy works ; for all the rare delights
Of eye and ear ; harmonious forms and strains
Of deepest breath, for each ensuing spring,
With all its tender leaves and blossoming ;
And dainty smells that steam from dropping rains ;
For sunlit days, and silent, shining nights,
For youth, and mirth, and health, though dashed
          with smarts
(As luscious creams are tinged with bitterness) ;
For Hope—sweet Hope ! unconscious of alloy,
For peaceful thoughts, kind faces, loving hearts,
That suck out all the poison from distress ;
For all these gifts I offer gratitude and joy !

The books he brought to Montague Square reminded me of two that he had given, some years before, to my sister Cecilia and to me, when we were little girls, and had each hemmed six silk pocket-handkerchiefs for him. The book he gave to Cecilia was Mary Lamb's ' Mrs Leicester's School,' and the one he gave to me was Charles Lamb's ' Adventures of Ulysses.' It bears on its blank page the words, ' Victoria Novello, from her sincere friend, Charles Cowden-Clarke, 22d February 1819.' This, his first gift to me, is on the library shelf opposite to me as I write.

I ought to have mentioned that an exceptionally proud gratification was mine when I earned my first five-pound note (my salary was twenty pounds a year), and I lay with the precious morsel of paper all night under my pillow. Next morning I was kindly allowed a holiday, when I asked leave to go and take the note to my mother myself.

It gives me pleasure to record another and very special instance of my lady-employer's amiable consideration for me. Once she gave a grand ball at her house, and she presented me with a sprigged muslin frock, and dressed my hair with her own hands, in order that her young governess might appear prettily attired in the dancing-room.

When spring came round, a superlative treat was planned for me by Charles Cowden-Clarke, who asked my mother and me to meet at his modest London lodgings, that we might go with him to Covent Garden Theatre and hear the new opera of ' Oberon,' which had been composed expressly for the then manager there, Charles Kemble, in consequence of the marked success of the previous opera, 'Der Freischütz.' Permission was (with the usual indulgence I met with from Mrs Purcell) granted me to accept this invitation, and a most memorable event it proved to be. The meeting with my beloved mother, the reception by our sprightly host, the delicious April sunshine pouring through the green Venetian blinds, the fine engraving propped on the table for our inspection, began the harmonious entertainment most harmoniously. While he and I lingered near each other, looking together at the picture (it was a print from Raphael's 'School of Athens'), the young girl's heart learnt its own secret—that it had given itself entirely to him who was by her side. Then came the delight of witnessing the first night's performance of Carl Maria Weber's enchanting fairy opera, the composer himself appearing in the orchestra and conducting the music. First-rate singers, first-rate instrumentalists, first-rate painters (for Roberts and Stanfield contributed some of the fine, poetic scenes) combined to make that first night of 'Oberon' a never-to-be-forgotten occasion.

As the season advanced, my health gave way so visibly that my parents resolved to withdraw me from my situation, where the noise and fatigue inevitable upon the daily presence of five young children had produced overwhelming headaches and almost total loss of appetite. Their mamma was kind and attentive to me in a most unwonted degree of personal care from a lady in her position to a young girl in mine. She generally came into the room where I and my pupils took our early dinner, and more than once ordered something for me that she thought might tempt me to eat, always accompanying the meal by a special glass of wine to give me strength. But when all failed to restore me, and I was to leave her employment, she put the climax to her amiable conduct by telling me that if ever I resumed governess-ship, she hoped I would let her know, in order that she might have an opportunity of re-engaging me.

Sea air having been recommended for me, my father and mother took me, one of my brothers and one of my sisters, to a pretty spot called Little Bohemia, not far from Hastings, where we spent many weeks, taking early plunges in the sea of a morning, long walks during the day, and pleasant talks in the evening. My brother Alfred was fond of being read to, therefore I usually had a book in my hand as we wandered through the pleasant neighbourhood, and read to him many an amusing or interesting narrative. Hollington Wood, Old Roar, etc., etc., were the scenes of our rambles, and much we enjoyed them in their rural beauty. That summer there was a very singular blight, or rather two blights. One was a visitation of the minutest black insects, who settled on our necks, shoulders, arms, faces—in short, wherever the skin was uncovered and allowed them to settle upon it. The other blight was inimical to the first blight, being no other than myriads of ladybirds, who devoured the black insects and swarmed to such an extent on all the vegetation around that every twig of the hedges looked like branches of reddest coral.

By the time we returned to Shacklewell, I was wonderfully improved in health, so much had I benefited by my summer at the seaside and by the exercise in the

open air which I had been able to take.
Life was very bright to me. Charles Cowden-Clarke came oftener and oftener down
from town to see us, and when he could
not come, he would send a letter to Bruns-
wick Square, where my father taught on
Tuesdays and Fridays at Miss Campbell's
school for twenty-seven years. Happy the
girl whose letters from and to the man
she prefers are conveyed by her own father.
Our mutual sympathy became more and
more confirmed, until on the 1st of
November that year (1826) we were
affianced to each other. I, being so young
—only seventeen—he had first written to
my parents, asking their approval of his
suit and their consent to his making
known to me his wish that I should become his wife, knowing how truly I should
be glad he took this course of appealing
to them first. They, esteeming and loving
him as they did, were rejoiced to learn
this prospect of happiness for their daughter,
and gave him their cordial consent.

The first walk in London that my
Charles and I took together after this
event, we went to Leicester Square, where
dwelt a pleasant old jeweller, Mr Chandler,
who knew us Novellos well, his acquaintance with our family dating from the time
when he had had friendly intercourse with
my maternal grandfather, and ever since,
whatever trinket-purchasing or trinket-
mending was needed, Mr Chandler was
applied to. Now, I was taken thither in
order to choose an engagement ring, and
I remember old Mr Chandler's roguish
smile and remark when he perceived that
I tried it on the third finger of my left
hand. The ring was a very simple one—
a half-hoop of garnets—for knowing that
my betrothed was not a rich man, I stipu-
lated that it should not be a costly ring ;
but it was a charming one to me, and Mr
Chandler told us it had been faceted by
a clever diamond-cutter. He was, according to his wont, full of entertaining
and intelligent chat, and among other

curiosities showed us Queen Elizabeth's watch, which was of the thickness of clasped hands.

In the course of that day's walk, we passed several shops where Charles wanted to enter and buy various knacks for me ; but I exercised my new right of despotic authority, and forbade him to squander his money, which I hoped he would hoard, as I intended to begin helping him to economise henceforth. I resumed, more warmly than ever, my desire to earn some contribution to our family income, as it was my parents' kind promise that I, as well as this new well-loved member thereof, should continue to reside with them after our marriage. Meanwhile, they removed from Shacklewell to No. 22 Bedford Street, Covent Garden, and it was here that I made my first attempt in literary production. My only confidant was my sister Cecilia. I wrote one short paper, entitled ' My Arm Chair,' signed merely ' M. H.' These initials I meant to represent 'Mary Howard,' because my father had, in his juvenile days, enacted the part of Sir John Falstaff as Mr Howard at some private theatricals. I sent my paper to the office where Hone's 'Table Book' was published, and to my great joy, and to that of my sister-confidant, my paper was promptly accepted, making its appearance in an early subsequent number of that interesting periodical. To figure in the same volumes where dear and honoured Charles Lamb was contributing his selections from 'The Garrick Plays' was in itself a greatly-to-be-prized distinction, but my happiest triumph was when I showed the paper to my Charles, telling him it was written by a girl of seventeen, and watched his look of pleased surprise when I told him *who* that girl was. I may here mention that this contribution of mine to Hone's 'Table Book' was followed by five others, respectively entitled, 'My Desk,' 'My Home,' 'My Pocket-Book,' 'Inn Yards,' and a paper on the '*Assignats*' in currency at the time of the French Republic of 1792. The paper was headed by a printed facsimile of an '*Assignat di dix sous*,' from one that had been given to me by my kind old tutor, Monsieur Bonnefoy.

A very delightful visit to the West of England was the one I made that summer to Mrs John Clarke (who, after the loss of her husband, had gone to live at Frome, in Somersetshire, with her unmarried youngest daughter) in order that I might make the acquaintance of my future mother-in-law. Her married daughter, Mrs Towers, resided at some miles distant from her, at Standerwick. It was to Mrs Towers that Charles Lamb addressed the following pleasant sonnet, written in her album :—

'Lady Unknown, who crav'st from me, Unknown,
The trifle of a verse these leaves to grace,
How shall I find fit matter ? with what face
Address a face that ne'er to me was shown ?
Thy looks, tones, gestures, manners and what not,
Conjecturing, I wander in the dark.
I know thee only sister to Charles Clarke !
But at that name my cold Muse waxes hot,

And swears that thou art such a one as he ;
Warm, laughter-loving, with a touch of madness,
Wild, glee-provoking, pouring oil of gladness
From frank heart without guile.   And if thou be
The pure reverse of this, and I mistake—
Demure one, I will like thee for his sake.'

She was the authoress of three books for
young people, 'The Children's Fireside,'
'The Young Wanderer's Cave,' and 'The
Adventures of Tom Starboard,' and in Leigh
Hunt's 'Literary Examiner' for December
13th, 1823, appeared her clever 'Stanzas to
a Fly that had survived the Winter of 1822.'

My reception by Charles's mother was
all that I could have hoped of affectionate
cordiality. It was evident that she 'took
to me' (as the phrase is) at once. She had
a way of putting her hand upon my knee
caressingly, when I sat by her side and she
talked to me, a token of liking that Charles
told me he had never seen her give, excepting
to one young lady whom she had known,
and was very fond of, in the old Enfield
times.   Curiously enough, she more than

once inadvertently called me by that young
lady's name instead of my own, as if I
somehow reminded her of the girl she had
so much loved.

At first, when evening came, Mrs Clarke
used to leave her youngest daughter in one
parlour to receive the visit of a neighbouring
gentleman to whom Eliza was engaged, while
Charles and I were left in the other parlour,
with the idea that the two couples of lovers
might like to be sole company for each
other ; but very soon Charles and I went
upstairs to fetch down his mother, as we told
her we could not afford to lose so many
hours of her society, now that we had come
on purpose to be as much with her as possible.
But she made us go out of mornings to
enjoy rambles in the picturesque vicinity ;
one of our frequent resorts being the lovely
park of Orchard Leigh. Here it was so
peaceful, and so much to ourselves, that the
cows used to come up and look at us as
strange beings who had wandered there they
knew not how, and who were too quietly

occupied with each other to need being any farther noticed.

One of the very earliest excursions planned for us by Charles's mother was a drive over to Standerwick. On our way thither we passed through the Marquis of Bath's beautiful estate—Long Leat. It so chanced that while the carriage ran by the side of a broad sheet of water there, we had a rare and interesting sight. A pair of swans rose from the lake and took flight to a short distance, affording the seldom-seen view of swans in the air.

On reaching the dwelling of the Towers family, Mrs Towers entered the room with her youngest child in her arms, beaming with smiles at our advent. She and her brother were warmly attached to each other, and the friendship she at once formed with his chosen future wife never ceased as long as she lived. In consequence of our having to return early to Frome, lunch was promptly laid on the table, and I recollect observing the tasteful mode in which it was arranged, with the exquisite effect of colouring pro-

D

duced by a large bowl of snowy curds and whey in contrast with a ruby-hued heap of gooseberry jam near it in the centre of the hospitable board. Mrs Towers was as famous for her home-made jams and other dulcet preparations as for her books and verses.

This visit to Charles's mother made me regret more than ever—as I had often regretted before—that I had never known his father. He had retired from the school at Enfield, and had gone to reside at Ramsgate before any meeting of our respective families had taken place ; but Charles always averred that he knew his father and I would have sympathised with each other intensely, and would have become fast friends. He was a man of nobly liberal opinions, of refined taste in literature, was as gentle-hearted as he was wise, and as wise as he was gentle-hearted. In his youth he had been articled to a lawyer at Northampton, and ran the risk of having to hang a man, in consequence of being deputed to fulfil the sheriff's office, because

Leigh Hunt

of the absence from town of the regularly-
appointed executioner. The whole night
was spent in an agony of mind by John
Clarke while endeavouring to find a substitute
for the task so inexpressibly repugnant to
him ; therefore, next morning, when he had
succeeded, he resolved there and then to
leave a situation that had subjected him to
so horrible a chance, and at once renounced
the legal profession—for which he had never
felt any liking—and adopted that of school-
master, for which he was eminently fitted.
He was always highly esteemed and affectionately regarded by his scholars, several of
whom, after they quitted his Enfield school,
became men of noted ability—John Keats,
Edward Cowper and Edward Holmes being
among the number.

Another visit of signal interest that year
was one that I paid to Mr and Mrs Leigh
Hunt, by their invitation, while they lived
at Highgate. I must have always had a
touch of romance in my disposition—even
as long back as when, quite a child, I had

crept round the sofa to kiss his hand, as
I have already recorded. Leigh Hunt, to
my imagination, had ever appeared an ideal
poet in visible form, and I regarded him
with a kind of idolatry, an enthusiasm of
reverential affection. Thus, to stay in the
same house with him, to be the companion
of his walks about such charming environs
as Hampstead, Caen Wood, Muswell Hill
and Freiern Barnet, to listen to his con-
fidential talk after breakfast, in his flowered
morning-gown, when he would discuss with
me his then literary projects in a style
which showed he felt he had near him one
who could thoroughly understand and appreciate his avowed views—all formed a bewitching combination that rendered this visit
indeed a memorable one to me. He was
then full of a project for writing a book
to be called 'Fabulous Zoology,' which was
to treat of dragons, griffins, cockatrices,
basilisks, etc., etc. He was also busy with
translations from French epigrammatic poets,
and he would murmur some happily-turned

line in the English rendering he contemplated
from Clement Marot or other similar author.
He had likewise a fancy for producing a
volume of fairy tales, one of which was
to be entitled 'Mother Fowl,' as a kind of
punning name for a heroine, reminding the
reader of 'Mother Goose,' only in this respect
—because 'Mother Fowl' was to have been
conspicuous for *foul*est dirty ways of mischief,
besides being grimiest of the grimy herself.

Having confessed to a touch of romance
in my disposition, I may here give an additional proof of its likelihood, by owning that
while Leigh Hunt was in Italy I had indulged girlish visions of the delight it would
be to me if I could gain a large fortune,
carry it thither myself, and lay it at his
feet. Again, when he returned thence to
England, and I chanced to hear him sing
one of Tom Moore's Irish melodies ('Rich
and rare were the gems she wore'), I was
so excited by the sound of his voice after
that lapse of time, that I found the tears
silently streaming down my cheeks.

Another visit, but of a very different kind, that year, was paid by my Charles and me together. He took me to see William Hone, who was then detained, by temporary money difficulties, 'within the rules' of the King's Bench Prison; so dingy and smoky were the regions through which we had to pass ere we arrived there, that a morsel of smut found its way to my face and stuck thereon during the first portion of our interview with Mr Hone. When Charles perceived the black intruder, he quickly puffed it off, and went on with his conversation. A day or two afterwards, when Hone again saw Charles, he said to him : 'You are engaged to Miss Novello, are you not?' 'What makes you think so?' was the reply. 'I saw you familiarly blow a smut off the young lady's face, to which familiarity she made no objection; therefore, I naturally guessed you were engaged to each other.' Hone's 'Table Book' had succeeded to his 'Every Day Book'; and it was to this last-named publication that Charles Lamb paid the gracefully - worded compliment in the concluding stanza of his lines to Hone :—

'Dan Phœbus loves your book—trust me, friend
    Hone—
  The title only errs, he bid me say ;
For while such art, wit, reading there are shown,
  He swears, 'tis not a work of *every day*.'

A similarly witty and elegant compliment was paid to his friend, Leigh Hunt, by Charles Lamb, in these lines that ended some he addressed to him at the time when each Wednesday brought out that delightful periodical called ' The Indicator ' :—

'I would not lightly bruise old Priscian's head,
  Or wrong the rules of grammar understood ;
But, with the leave of Priscian be it said,
  The *Indicative* is your *Potential Mood*.
Wit, poet, proseman, partyman, translator—
Hunt, your best title yet is *Indicator*.'

To this periodical my mother was god-mother. There had been some difficulty in finding a name for it ; and she not only suggested the one ultimately adopted, but she supplied the following passage—which formed

the heading of each number :—' There is a bird
in the interior of Africa whose habits would
rather seem to belong to the interior of Fairy-
land ; but they have been well authenticated.
It indicates to honey-hunters where the nests
of wild bees are to be found.   It calls them
with a cheerful cry, which they answer, and
on finding itself recognised, flies and hovers
over a hollow tree containing the honey.
While they are occupied in collecting it, the
bird goes to a little distance, where he ob-
serves all that passes ; and the hunters, when
they have helped themselves, take care to
leave him his portion of the food.   This is
the *Cuculus Indicator* of Linnæus, otherwise
the moroc, bee-cuckoo, or honey-bird.

> ' " Then he arriving round about doth flie
> And takes survey with busie, curious eye ;
> Now this, now that, he tasteth tenderly."
> > SPENSER.'

I cannot forbear quoting the concluding
droll paragraph of a short article that appeared in the first number of the ' Indicator,' on
the ' DIFFICULTY OF FINDING A NAME FOR A

WORK OF THIS KIND.' Leigh Hunt is de-
scribing a company of his friends helping
him by suggesting titles : 'Some of the names
had a meaning in their absurdity, such as
" The Adviser, or Helps for Composing " ;
" The Cheap Reflector, or Every Man His
Own Looking-Glass " ; " The Retailer, or Every
Man his Own Other Man's Wit " ; " Nonsense,
to be continued." Others were laughable by
the mere force of contrast, as " The Crocodile,
or Pleasing Companion " ; " Chaos, or the
Agreeable Miscellany"; "The Fugitive Guide";
" The Footsoldier, or Flowers of Wit " ;
"Bigotry, or the Cheerful Instructor " ; " The
Polite Repository of Abuse " ; " Blood, being
a Collection of Light Essays." Others were
sheer ludicrousness and extravagance, as "The
Pleasing Ancestor " ; " The Silent Remarker " ;
" The Tart " ; " The Leg of Beef, by a Lay-
man "; "The Ingenious Hatband "; "The Boots
of Bliss " ; " The Occasional Diner " ; " The
Toothache " ; " Recollections of a very Un-
pleasant Nature " ; "Thoughts on a Hill of
Considerable Eminence " ; " Meditations on a

Pleasing Idea " ; " Materials for Drinking " ;
" The Knocker, No. 1 " ; " The Hippo-
potamus, Entered at Stationer's Hall " ; " The
Pianoforte of Paulus Æmilius " ; " The Seven
Sleepers at Cards " ; " The Arabian Nights
on Horseback," with an infinite number of
other mortal murders of common sense, which
rose to " push us from our stools," and which
none but the wise or good-natured would
ever think of laughing at.'

.   .   .   .

In the next year to that of which I have
been writing, my parents removed from
Bedford Street to No. 66 Great Queen
Street, Lincoln's Inn Fields ; and Charles became urgent with them to let me fix a day for
our marriage. It took place with a quiet
simplicity that particularly pleased us both.
My dear father and mother were the only
persons with us when, early in the morning of 5th July 1828, we drove to Blooms-
bury Church. Two milkmaids chanced to
be standing near as we went up the steps,
and I heard one of them say : ' That's the

bride.' A neat white satin cottage bonnet
and a white muslin dress—both the work
of my own hands—were all the wedding
adornments that denoted me to them. A
sweet, peaceful solemnity was in the tran-
quilly-uttered words of the ceremony; but
the clerk, after the service, indulged in a
smile as he observed me about to sign my
new name in the register book, remarking
that many brides made this mistake, and
directing me to write, for the last time, my
maiden name. I remember rather wonder-
ing at my own perfect calmness during the
service, for I had determined not to follow
Charlotte Grandison's example of hesitation
at saying the word 'obey,' but to speak
'love, honour and obey' with the full tone
that should express the true wish of my
heart to faithfully keep this vow. Well
might I, with such a man as he was who
had chosen me, and whom I had long
known, esteemed, respected, admired and
warmly loved.

On our return we found breakfast ready

laid, certain of the plates having upon
them a gift each, which my mother had,
with her usual kind thought, provided for
the bride to present to her young brothers
and sisters. This pleasant meal and pre-
sentation being over, and the wedding-
dress exchanged for a thicker muslin and
plainer cottage bonnet of straw, we prepared to leave the dear home to which we
were soon to return. My mother's sweet,
penetrating voice followed us forth, uttering
the few but tender words, ' Take care of
her, Charley.' Be it here noted, that as
soon as Charles became one of the family
he was invariably called by that boyish
form of his name, proving how ever-young
was his nature to the last hour of his existence. He had decided upon making his
native Enfield our honeymoon quarters,
therefore we took our way to the Bell
Inn in Holborn, whence the Edmonton
stage-coach started. On our way thither
he laughingly told me of a man who had
said to his new-made wife an hour after

their espousals, 'Hitherto, madam, I have been your slave, now you are mine.' When we reached Edmonton we alighted from the coach, and crossed the stile beyond which were the fields that lie between that place and Enfield. Brilliant was the July sun, blue the sky, whereon dainty little white cloudlets appeared like tufts of swandown, scarcely moved by the light summer air. We lingered, leaning on the wooden railing that surmounted the miniature bridge over the rivulet, where Keats used to watch the minnows 'staying their wavy bodies 'gainst the streams,' and on along the 'footpath' which his 'friend Charles' had 'changed for the grassy plain,' when, on parting at night, between their respective homes, Keats says, 'I no more could hear your footsteps touch the gravelly floor.' The very words with which the young poet concluded this, his 'Epistle to Charles Cowden-Clarke,' seemed then and there to be fulfilling, for he goes on to say, 'In those still moments I have wish'd you joys

that well you know to honour,' and the
'joys' of that day certainly crowned with
reality the affectionate aspiration. Farther
on we went, entering the meadow skirted
by the row of sapling oaks planted by
Charles's father—the bag of acorns for the
purpose being carried by the little son—
until we came to the wall belonging to the
end of the schoolhouse garden, behind
which wall was an arbour where Charles
used to read to Keats Spenser's exquisite
'Epithalamion,' and where they talked poetry
together, the elder of the two introducing
the younger to the divine art, and 'first
taught him all the sweets of song,' finally
lending him Spenser's 'Fairie Queene,' to
Keats's infinite rapture. We took up our
abode at a rural hostelry called 'The Greyhound,' kept by a comfortable old man and
his daughter, named Powell. This hostelry
possessed a pleasant sitting-room overlooking 'the green' and its spreading oak
tree, and as pleasant a sleeping-room, with
its window screened by a vine trained

across it, casting a verdant, softened light
within. It was to the period of our
sojourn here that Charles Lamb referred
in a letter he afterwards wrote to Charles,
saying,—' When you lurked at " The Greyhound." Benedicks are close, but how I
so totally missed you at that time, going
for my morning cup of ale duly, is a
mystery. 'Twas stealing a match before
one's face in earnest. But certainly we
had not a dream of your propinquity. . . .
I promise you the wedding was very pleasant news to me, indeed.'

Enchanting were the daily long walks
we took, and enchanted ground seemed
the lovely English rural lanes and meadows
we passed through, visiting all the most
notable points around that vicinity, so
dearly associated as it was to us. Often
did we turn at once into the roadway
where the charming old schoolhouse
stood (it was under a stranger's mastership
now), and look up at its curious front
of rich red brick, moulded into designs re-

presenting garlands of flowers and pome-
granates, together with heads of Cherubim,
over two niches in the centre of the
building, which, on one of its bricks, bore
the figures 1717. This frontage was, indeed, esteemed so curious and interesting
as a specimen of bygone English domestic
architecture, that when, subsequently, the
schoolhouse was bought for a railway
station the company kept the front carefully, and it was preserved in the
exhibition buildings of the Kensington
Museum, where I had the pleasure of
seeing it when I visited England many
years afterwards.

Between the 'two niches' just mentioned,
there was the window of a room in which,
during some childish illness, Charles had
been put to sleep apart from the other
boys, and the little fellow—thinking this
a capital opportunity—had crept out on
to the lead flat over the entrance door,
that he might properly and closely inspect
the pomegranate garlands and Cherubim,

which he had heard extolled by his elders.

Opposite to the schoolhouse was a bend of the New River, in neighbouring portions of which winding stream Charles and his schoolfellows had enjoyed many a luxurious plunge, and, after bathing, had disdained to use towels, but dried themselves by scampers over the grassy fields close to its shores. Farther on, beyond the schoolhouse, the road led beneath a small wooded acclivity, but large enough to have allowed Charles, when a young lad, to imagine it a forest peopled with dragons, lions, ladies, knights, dwarfs and giants, while he gazed at this spot from a window which commanded a view of it. The road terminated at a place called Ponder's End, but as it possessed no particular interest we generally made this the returning point.

Other days we took the exactly opposite direction, going past the house where Richard Warburton Lytton (grandfather of Lytton Bulwer, afterwards Lord Lytton) resided.

E

He had been very kind to Charles when quite a young boy, lending him books and talking pleasantly to him while taking exercise on what was then called a ' chamber-horse.'

Proceeding farther, we came to a house with a garden, that had a pond abutting on the road. In this pond were some beautiful water-lilies in full bloom, and we always used to stop and look at them ; for it so chanced that they were the first I had ever seen. Then we came to a stile, giving entrance to a series of delicious green fields, which were exchanged for a path through a small wood, then more fields, until we reached Winchmore Hill. The exceeding beauty of this district had been charmingly described by Charles, in a short paper called 'Walks round London,' No. 1, which appeared in Leigh Hunt's 'Literary Pocket Book,' or 'Companion for the Lovers of Nature and Art,' in the year 1820.

Sometimes we wandered as far as Theobald's Park and White-Webb's Wood, tra-

ditionally said to be the place where the con-
spirators in James the First's reign used to
meet. My remembrance of it is that of a
quiet, umbrageous spot, delightful for a rest
after a pedestrian ramble. Very frequently
we made our way back, from one of these
walks, to our hostelry, along a rustic path
which ran parallel with the chief street of
Enfield ; partly because it was more tranquil
and retired, partly because it was more shady,
and lastly, because it was near to a rookery,
which had peculiar attraction for us, being
the abode of birds, watched of an evening
by Charles and his schoolfellows, who
used to look up and shout to the black
train as it came home to roost, ' Lag,
lag, laglast ! ' Once, however, we were
startled by the report of a gun, and saw
some dark object fall, that reminded us of
the feathered victim of Caspar's magic
shot in Weber's ' Freischütz ' ; but it was
probably some harmless gamekeeper occupied in the discharge of his duty.

On our return to town we were

welcomed to our parents' home, making it happily ours in every sense of the word, and it continued thus wherever their domicile might be situated. For twenty years we enjoyed that privilege of living with them—a privilege as delightful as rare.

Ere quite settling down, Charles Lamb invited us to spend a week with him and his sister (who were then living at Chaseside, Enfield), to make amends for our having 'lurked at "The Greyhound,"' when he 'had not a dream of our propinquity.' How fully and delightfully that visit enabled us to behold him in his individuality of whimsical humour as well as his thoroughly tender and kind nature. His lifelong devotion to his sister had been practically proved ; but his mingled playfulness of treatment and manner towards her were indicated in his once saying to us, with his arch smile, 'I always call my sister Maria when we are alone together, Mary when we are with friends, and Moll before the servants.'

He was as fond of long walks as we were,

and had equal admiration for Enfield and its
environs as we had. He showed us the very
spot where a dog had been pertinacious in
following him, and whom he sought to get
rid of by *tiring him out (!)*, had given up the
contest of perseverance, and had dropped
down under a hedge dead beat. He took
us to Cheshunt and to Northaw, with the
hope of finding a famous old giant oak tree
we had severally heard was to be seen at one
or other of these places ; but the search was
vain in both cases. The disappointment was
small, but the pleasure of the walks infinite.
On one especial occasion, when Fanny Kelly
chanced to come down from London to see
the Lambs at Chaseside when we were there,
a walk was proposed which took us past a
picturesque ford, at a little distance from a
wayside waggon-inn. Beside this country
inn were pleasant shady seats, and Lamb
proposed we should tarry awhile and rest.
Neither Fanny Kelly nor we two declining the proposal, but glad to please him, and
glad to have the pleasure of sitting there with

him and his sister, and the delightful actress, we loitered, leisurely sipping our draughts of malt, in a companionship most pleasant to me to remember. By-the-bye, I may record that I won Charles Lamb's increase of esteem (on some occasion when I was speaking of my father's having made me at rare times acquainted with that 'Lutheran Beer,' porter, alluded to in Elia's 'Chapter on Ears') by saying that I preferred Barclay & Perkins's brewage to Whitbread's, or any other brewers that I had ever tasted. He was fond of testing people's capacity for understanding his mode of indulging in odd, bluntish speeches, but which contained a certain quaint evidence of familiar liking. Once, when we were returning from a walk, and Mary Lamb took the opportunity of calling in to make some purchases she needed at a village linendraper's shop near Winchmore Hill, her brother, standing by with us, addressed the mistress of the shop in a tone of pretended sympathy, saying : ' I hear that trade's falling off, Mrs Udall, how's this?' The stout,

cheery woman only smiled and answered good-
humouredly, for it was evident that she was
acquainted with Charles Lamb's whimsical
way, he being familiarly known at the shops
where his sister dealt.

Another time, during this visit to the
Lambs, he had given his arm to me, and left
my husband to escort Miss Lamb, who walked
at rather more slow a pace than her brother,
while we were going to spend the evening at
the house of a somewhat prim lady school-mis-
tress. On entering the room, Charles Lamb
introduced me to this rather formal hostess
with the words, ' Mrs ———, I've brought
you the wife of the man who mortally hates
your husband,' and when the lady replied by
a polite inquiry after Miss Lamb, hoping she
was quite well, Charles Lamb said, ' She has
a terrible fit of toothache this evening, so Mr
Cowden-Clarke remained to keep her company.' Soon after this, the two appearing,
Lamb went on to say, ' Mrs Cowden-Clarke
has been telling me, as we came along, that
she hopes you have sprats for supper.' The

lady's puzzled look, contrasted by the smiling calmness with which we stood by listening to him, were precisely the effects that amused Lamb to produce. I have heard him say that he never stammered when he told a lie. This was in humorous reference to the slight hesitation in his speech which he often had when talking.

On the last evening of this delightful visit, Charles Lamb (who was fond of whist and had asked us whether we were good hands at the game, we disclaiming any such excellence, had brought his rejoinder of, 'Oh, then, I'll not ask you to play ; I hate playing with bad players') said, 'Let's have a game of whist, just to see what you are like ; ' and at the end of the trial he burst out with, 'If I had known you could play as well as this, we would have had whist every evening.'

He was the cordialest of hosts—playful, genial, hospitably promotive of pleasureable things, walks, cheerful meals, and the very best of talk. It had been said of him that he always said the best thing of the evening, when even the finest spirits of the time met together. His hospitality, while we were visiting him that memorable week, the incidents of which I have been recording, was characteristically manifested one day, in his own peculiarly whimsical way, by his starting up from dinner, hastening to the front garden gate, and opening it for a donkey, who he saw standing there, and looking, as Lamb said, as if it wanted to come in and munch some of the grass growing so plentifully behind the railing.

When we returned home to enter upon our intended course of life, my Charles at once made himself truly one of the family, taking a brotherly interest in Alfred's preparations for soon beginning business as a music-seller ; in Edward's attendance at Mr Sass's School of Design, having shown decided talent for drawing, and possessing an ardent desire for becoming an artist ; in Clara's already manifest vocal ability (she was but three years old when she startled her parents by singing correctly the tune of ' *Di tanti palpiti*,' which she had merely heard played on a barrel-organ in the street ; and I often afterwards used to see my father call her to the piano, with her doll in her arms, to sing some song of Handel's or Mozart's that he had taught her, while still a mere child) ; and in the lessons of the two youngest girls, which lessons Charles gave them himself. The two children used to lie down on the carpet, one on each side of his chair, with their slates and their books before them, while he continued his own writing, until his little pupils should be ready to repeat the lessons they had learned.

He busied himself with the articles he had to write for the 'Atlas' newspaper, on the staff of which he was engaged for notices of the 'Fine Arts.' And with papers on 'Theatricals' for the 'Examiner' newspaper. This latter-named engagement afforded us most congenial entertainments for our evenings, since it took us perpetually to the different theatres, sometimes having to go to two of them on the same evening—perhaps a new comedy at Drury Lane or Covent

Garden, followed by a new farce at the Haymarket or Lyceum.   Not being able to afford
a cab, we used to trudge on foot to each of
these appointed houses, Charles with his dress
coat and waistcoat covered by a cloak, I with
'full dress,' needed for the 'Dress Circle,'
similarly enveloped.   Heartily did we enjoy
these necessary economies ; as, indeed, then
and long afterwards we did, during the period
when they had to be practised.   Mutual
esteem and passionate attachment made
poverty (or perhaps I should say very small
means) seem scarcely an evil, but, on the
contrary, something to be cheerfully and
willingly borne, being borne together and
for the sake of each other.   Moreover, we
had the blessing of generously kind parents,
who let us contribute our share of the household expenses at such convenient periods
as best suited our earned receipts.   These
were added to by Charles's acceptance of a
thoroughly uncongenial post as editor of, and
writer in, a periodical entitled 'The Reper-
tory of Patent Inventions.'   But he and we

all took refuge from the dryness of the task
by making it the subject of constant laughter
and jest in our family circle. Not one of us
read it ; not one of us cared even to look at
it, save on a single occasion, when Charles,
having indulged himself by writing a rather
facetious article on some heavy, newly-in-
vented manufacture, was rebuked by a com-
munication from a person signing himself
'Fairy' (of all names in the world!) for
writing so *lightly* on such a weightily important theme ! To recur to the pleasanter
subject of the theatrical notices Charles had
to write, and the theatre-goings they involved
for us both. We had before then had the
good fortune to see the very best acting ; that
of Edmund Kean, Dowton, Munden, Liston,
the elder Mathews, Miss Kelly, Mrs Daven-
port, etc. The first named I had seen in his
rarely performed part of Luke, in a play
called 'Riches,' and also as Sir Giles Overreach in Massinger's 'A New Way to pay
Old Debts.' As Luke I remember his entrance while supposed to be desperately poor

—his head bent, his whole frame stooping, his clothes of the meanest, and bearing beneath his arms and dependent from his hands various bundles he had been ordered to carry. Of his Sir Giles Overreach I chiefly remember the death-scene. Kean lay prostrate near to the footlights, his face and figure clearly visible to the audience, and fearfully true to the ebbing of life was the picture they presented. In 'Othello,' a striking point was the mode in which he clung to the side scene when uttering the words, 'Not a jot, not a jot,' in Act iii. Scene 3, as if trying to steady himself against the heart-blow he was receiving. Towards the latter portion of his career, Kean most frequently played Shylock, and grand was his playing throughout. But a superb piece of action and voice was his, as he delivered the speech, concluding with the words—'The villainy you teach me, I will execute; and it shall go hard, but I will better the instruction.' He seemed positively to writhe from head to foot as he poured forth his anguished recapitulation of his own

and his nation's wrongs, of his deadly hatred
of the wrongers, and of his as deadly deter-
mination to have his revenge upon them.
Dowton's great part of Dr Cantwell in 'The
Hypocrite' (Cibber's translated version of
Molière's 'Tartuffe') was impressed upon
my memory, if only by the tone of his voice
—subdued, would-be meek, while Cantwell is
sustaining the appearance of prone devotion—
and the insolent loudness of the tone, when,
the mask thrown off, he proclaims himself
master of the house and all its inmates.   In
the first place he calls to Sir John Lambert's
Secretary, softly and mildly, 'Charles!' in
utter contrast with the mode in which he
roughly and peremptorily calls out to him,
in the latter case, 'Seyward!' The two so
remarkably differing tones still seem to reach
my ears as I write.

Munden could be impressive in grave
characters as well as great in ultra-comic
power, celebrated by Charles Lamb in his
Elia paper, entitled 'On the Acting of
Munden.' Besides seeing him in old 'Cockle-

top' and in 'Crack the Cobbler,' I witnessed
his admirable performance of old Dornton
in the 'Road to Ruin'—a perfect gentleman
in bearing and conduct, a sorrowful father
grieved by his son's indiscretions. His very
commencement in the opening scene—'Past
two o'clock and Harry not yet returned'—
rings touchingly even now upon my hearing,
accompanied as the words were by the sad
and anxious look upon his face while drawing the watch from its fob. Liston, the
inimitable, also could be excellent in pathetic
parts, although so famed for his surpassing
comic performances. He, too, had been written
of by Charles Lamb, who, in one instance,
wrote what he named 'The Biographical
Memoir of Mr Liston'—absurdly fictitious
but certainly most humorous. The character
I saw him play, where he had one scene of
profound pathos, was Russet, in Colman's
play of 'The Jealous Wife.' The father's
agony, when he fears that his daughter has
been carried off by a libertine young man,
amounted to the tragic in its storm of

mingled rage and grief. Few witnessing his
power of serious acting in that scene could
believe that a man who so often made them
burst into roars of laughter was one and
the same individual. I heard that Liston
once laid a wager with Kean (who had said
that nothing could disturb his seriousness
while on the stage) that he could succeed in
making him laugh even there. Once, when
Kean was playing Rolla, a procession of veiled
Virgins of the Sun had to enter and pass
before him. The first virgin, as she passed,
suddenly raised her veil, confronted Kean
with the irresistible visage of Liston, and
the wager was won, for Kean went off into
an incontrollable fit of laughter. We used
not infrequently to meet Mr and Mrs Liston
at the Lambs' apartments while they lived
in Russell Street, Covent Garden ; and I
once heard Mrs Liston sing. It was in a
small operatic afterpiece. She had a very
sweet voice, a fair complexion, and a dump-
ling figure, which caused some wag to say
she looked like a fillet of veal upon castors.

Another of our early dramatic treats had
been seeing the elder Mathews in his celebrated 'Entertainments,' in which he not only
represented one, but often several different
personages. There was a scene, where two
burglars were supposed to be stealing into a
house with intention to rob. So quickly
were the changes of garment effected, while
passing behind a screen, or darting swiftly
and noiselessly off and on the side scenes,
so amazingly well altered were the manner,
voice and look of the two thieves that it was
scarcely possible to believe them to be the
same individual. A scene in another of these
'Entertainments' was a London street at
night, where a watchman's box occupied the
centre of the stage. Mathews, as an old
watchman, entered, and after a grumbling
speech went into his box to have a cosy nap.
Then, successively, came along the front of
the stage some of the actors most popular
in that day, supposed to be returning home
after the night's performance at the theatre.
Even now I can hear the intonation of Kean's

F

voice and imitation of his look as given by
Mathews while passing before the watch-box ;
then Braham, then Liston and several others
followed, all equally 'done to the life' by
the wonderfully accurate mimic. One of
his most famous impersonations in still
another of these 'Entertainments' was an
old Scotchwoman. garrulous and full of anecdote ; and yet another—a father of a family
conducting his youngsters through the illuminated marvels of Vauxhall Gardens, perpetually slapping and cuffing them to keep
them in order before him, and calling out—
'Keep together ! keep together, I tell you !
I brought you out to make you happy, why
can't you keep together ? '

During the time of our theatre-goings
after marriage, we still saw delightful dramas,
wherein Kean, Dowton, Munden, etc., were
the chief performers at Drury Lane and
Covent Garden, while at the other houses
we had the gratification of witnessing many
'First Nights' of peculiar interest. Charles's
engagement to write the theatrical notices

of course afforded peculiar opportunity for this privilege. Thus we were present when several of Douglas Jerrold's plays came out— his 'Housekeeper,' 'Nell Gwynne,' 'The Prisoner of War,' 'Time Works Wonders,' etc., and we had the pleasure of seeing the author himself in the principal character of his 'Painter of Ghent,' when he played it for the first few nights. We saw Liston's first appearance in Poole's 'Paul Pry,' at once making a prodigious 'hit.' At the Olympic we were among the audience when Madame Vestris appeared as 'Orpheus,' clad in the smallest amount of clothing I had ever *then* seen worn upon the stage. Her figure was perfection. She looked like an exquisite Greek statue. In a shop window in Oxford Street there used to be seen a sandal of Madame Vestris's, her foot being renowned for its small size and great beauty.

Our evenings at the theatres brought us frequently into companionship with that super-excellent critic, William Hazlitt, who was likewise occupied in writing theatrical notices

—those for the ' Times' newspaper. It was always a treat to sit beside him, when he talked delightfully ; and once, on going to his own lodging, he showed us a copy he had made of Titian's 'Ippolito dei Medici,' and conversed finely upon Titian's genius. Hazlitt's gift in painting was remarkable. A portrait he took of his old nurse—a mere head, the upper part of the face in strong shadow from an over-pending black silk bonnet edged with black lace, while the wrinkled cheeks, the lines about the mouth, with the touches of actual and reflected light, were given with such vigour and truth as might well recall the style of the renowned Flemish master, and actually did cause a good judge of the art to say to Hazlitt— ' Where did you get that Rembrandt ? '

At the theatre we frequently beheld Godwin, with his eyes fixed upon the stage, his arms folded across his chest, while his glistening bald head—which somebody had said was entirely without the organ of veneration—made him conspicuous even at a

distance ; and similarly beheld was Horace
Smith, whose profile bore a remarkable likeness to that of Socrates (as known to us
through traditional delineation), and whose
' Rejected Addresses ' were so admiringly and
risibly known to us.

When the first anniversary of our wedding
came round, Charles and I indulged ourselves with accepting his sister's invitation
to spend a fortnight's visit to her and her
family at Standerwick. A pleasant and even
memorable time it was to us. The house
stood near to a wooded spot, where we
could hear a certain kind of thrush, called
a storm-cock, sing the whole day long, with
a perseverance native to him, perched on the
top of a high tree. Mr and Mrs Towers,
delightfully hospitable and intent upon
making our stay in every way delightful to
us, taking us charming walks to see all the
most picturesque spots around them, and
furnishing the most interesting topics of
conversation, versed as they both were in
literature ; while Mr Towers was an enthu-

siastic lover of music, no mean performer
on the pianoforte himself, besides being skilful and practical in chemistry. It was at
their breakfast-table one morning that regret
was expressed with regard to there being no
Concordance to Shakespeare in existence.
Eagerly, as is my nature, I immediately resolved that I would undertake this work,
and, accordingly, when after breakfast a
walk was proposed over to Warminster, I
took with me a volume of Shakespeare, a
pencil and paper, and jotted down my plan,
beginning with the first line of my intended
book. During our walk we chanced to pass
an enclosure where some sea-gulls were kept
and were screaming loudly. I have never
heard that sound since, but I have associated
it with that day of commencing my sixteen
years' work.

Besides his theatrical and fine art notices,
Charles busied himself with writing some
books he had in hand. One was a tasteful
boy's book, called 'Adam the Gardener';
another was his beautifully-rendered 'Tales

from Chaucer,' and a third named 'Nyren's Cricketer's Guide,' which was the result of putting into readable form the recollections of a vigorous old friend who had been a famous cricketer in his youth and early manhood, and who, in his advanced age, used to come and communicate his cricketing experiences to Charles with chuckling pride and complacent reminiscence.

It was in this same year of 1829 that my father and mother took a journey to Germany for the purpose of conveying to Mozart's sister, Madame Sonnenberg (who was then out of health and in poor circumstances), a sum of money which had been subscribed by some musical admirers of her brother's genius. My father had been the originator of this subscription, and undertook all its contingent expenses himself; therefore, it was with pleased zeal that he went on this expedition to Salzburg. He kept a diary during its progress, and records with enthusiasm its incidents. Extracts from this diary are given in my 'Life and Labours of Vincent Novello.

Ere the close of the year, Madame Sonnenberg died, and Vincent Novello crowned his tribute of respect to her by getting up a performance of her illustrious brother's 'Requiem,' with organ accompanied by few but choice instruments and voices. It so chanced that the interesting performance was the one which terminated the renowned series that had rendered South Street Chapel so attractive to musical hearers; for soon after it was closed, and the Portuguese Embassy no longer had services there.

It was on their way back from Germany that my parents achieved the accomplishment of their desire to place their daughter Clara in the Academy of Singing for church music at Paris, where Monsieur Choron was headmaster of the establishment. My father called upon him and obtained leave for Clara to enter herself as candidate at the approaching election which was to take place, a vacancy for a pupil there presenting itself. My mother, with her usual energetic decision and prompt activity, immediately set

out to fetch Clara in time for the day of
trial. On the eve, one of those who were
to be her judges chancing to hear her re-
hearsing, thought it must be a girl of at
least fifteen to whom he listened, so fine
was her style, so round and full was her
tone. Her father had taught her so well,
and had so accustomed her to execute Handel's noblest sacred songs, as well as Mozart's
and other operatic composers' arias, that she
was thoroughly versed in them. Therefore,
next day, when she went through her ordeal,
she was as unperturbed and calm as if she
were at home ; yet she was so child-like
and small of stature that she had to be
placed upon a low stool in order to be seen
by her umpires, and she had attained so few
summers of life, that the self-possession and
ability with which she sang the ' Agnus
Dei ' from Mozart's Mass in F., No. 1,
and Dr Arne's, ' The Soldier tired,' caused
her to be unanimously pronounced the successful candidate against nineteen competi-
tors. That calm self-possession, when she

sang, lasted always; and her voice in its silvery sweetness, with potency of tone, exists still at her now advanced age. Her artistic career was a series of brilliant successes (among them was her having been received by the respective sovereigns at their courts of Windsor, Berlin and St Petersburg with even kindly graciousness); and her domestic life since has been a very happy one.

About this period my father removed from Great Queen Street to No. 67 Frith Street, where his son Alfred was to begin business as a music-seller. Very modest was the shop-front—merely a couple of parlour windows and a glass door displaying a few title-pages bearing composers' names of sterling merit, with Vincent Novello's as editor; but this simple beginning led to an eminent result—that of a sacred music warehouse universally dealt with by the musical world. It affords a striking example of the success that attends genuine love of art and zeal in promoting the diffusion of its means for cultivation on the part of him who edited, together with industry, punctuality and regularity on the part of the young publisher, aided as they were by the practical counsel and moral encouragement of her who devoted herself to the chief aims of her husband and son—indeed, of all her children. On the evening of the 15th February 1830, my Charles and I were at the Lyceum Theatre, where a French company were giving performances. We saw Potier, a celebrated comedian, play in ' Le Chiffonier,' and ' Le Cuisinier de Buffon.' A few hours after we left the theatre it was burnt to the ground. My brothers, Alfred and Edward, awakened by the glare in the sky, jumped out of their beds and ran off to see the conflagration. When they recounted at breakfast-time what had happened during the night, it may be imagined how fervent was our gratitude at having escaped so great a peril.

Not long after that event my husband and I spent a wonderful hour with Coleridge.

Charles had been requested by his acquaintance, Mr Edmund Reade, to take a message
for him to the venerable poet, respecting a
poem lately written by Mr Reade, called
' Cain.' Rejoiced were we to have this
occasion for a visit to Coleridge, who then
resided at Highgate, in Mr Colman's house,
and who had formerly been known to
Charles at Ramsgate, through Charles
Lamb's introduction. When I was introduced to him as Vincent Novello's eldest
daughter, Coleridge was struck by my
father's name, knowing it to be that of a
musician, and forthwith plunged into a
fervid and eloquent praise of music, branch-
ing into explanation of an idea he had,
that the creation of the universe must have
been accompanied by a grand prevailing
harmony of spheral music.

In that same spring we saw Fanny Kemble
play Portia in ' The Merchant of Venice ' for
her first benefit. We had been in the house
the previous autumn when she made her *début*
on the stage in the character of Juliet ; her

mother, Mrs Charles Kemble, reappearing, for
that night only, as Lady Capulet, Mrs Daven-
port acting the nurse, and Charles Kemble,
Mercutio. The enthusiasm of the public was
naturally great, for it was known that the
young *débutante* had chosen the dramatic
profession in the hope of saving the for-
tunes of the theatre, then at a low ebb and
under the lesseeship of her father, while the
reappearance of her mother created additional
interest. It seems but yesterday that we saw
the real tears flowing down Mrs Charles
Kemble's cheeks at the hearty welcome of
applause that greeted her from the audience,
or beheld the animated entrance of Charles
Kemble as he sprang forward at the commencement of Act ii. with the elasticity of
youth, although we heard that he was then
past sixty years of age. He was one of the
most gracefully vivacious of actors in characters that required personal attraction and
charm of manner. His Archer in the 'Beaux
Stratagem,' where a gentleman undertakes
to pass for a footman, was so unmistakably

the former, while paying court to a lady in
gaily free style, that no wonder Mrs Sullen
finds him well-nigh irresistibly polished and
winning in speech and manner. His Captain
Absolute, his Benedick, his Faulconbridge,
his Cassio, were all perfect, and we had the
pleasure of seeing him in all these characters.
As Cassio, I remember my father saying that,
in Scene 2, Act iii., of 'Othello,' Charles
Kemble looked like a drunken man trying
to appear sober, instead of a sober man trying
to look drunk, as many actors do. As Faulconbridge he seemed the embodiment of
English chivalry, while in the scene with
his mother, Lady Faulconbridge, his manly
tenderness, his filial coaxing way of speaking
and putting his arm round her as he thanks
her for having made Richard Cœur de Lion
his father, was something to be grateful for
having witnessed. No one but Elliston
could compete with Charles Kemble for his
supremely winning mode of enacting a
wooer. We saw Fanny Kemble many
times and in her best parts, thinking so

well of her acting that we found it strange
when, years afterwards, we read her slighting
mention of herself as a performer.   Certainly
her Julia in Sheridan Knowles's play of 'The
Hunchback' was a piece of nobly-conceived
and executed impersonation, while the way
in which she looked and acted the queen-
mother in her own play of 'Francis the First'
was quite admirable.   That a young girl
of fifteen should have written that strong
play was in itself a patent proof of her
innate strength and talent with keen perception of dramatic fitness.

The second anniversary of our wedding day
was spent delightfully at Cambridge.   My
father had been asked by the authorities of
the Fitzwilliam Museum there to examine
the large collection of musical manu-
scripts in their library ; and he accordingly
visited Cambridge many times at his own
expense for that purpose.   On this occasion he
made his visit a family holiday, taking with
him his wife, his son Edward, my Charles and
me.   Much of his time was spent in making

copies of some of these MSS., chiefly those by masters of the ancient Italian school, such as Buononcini, Clari, Carissimi, Leo, Martini, Palestrina, Stradella, etc., and some of these MSS. were subsequently printed and published by him under the name of 'The Fitzwilliam Music.'

My brother Edward had made such good use of his studies under Mr Sass, and had worked so diligently at home, practising in oils as well as in water-colours, that he made use of his visit to Cambridge by taking copies of some of the fine pictures in the Fitzwilliam Museum. His beautiful copy of Rembrandt's 'Dutch Officer' (life size) and of Annibale Caracci's 'St Roch and the Angel' were the result of his painting there, and are still among our preserved treasures that we owe to him in the picture-gallery of our present Italian home. Edward's steady perseverance and industry—more or less characterising all my father's children, and inherited from him — existed in a remark-

able degree in our young artist. He
was scarcely ever without a paint-brush
in his hand during the day ; and of an
evening, when reading aloud was going
on, he had always pen and pencil before
him, wherewith he made sketches of the
various characters in the books thus perused. His original pictures are several :—
My father's portrait (a perfect likeness)
my mother's, my sister Clara's, his own
face, wearing various expressions ; ' Illustrations to my Charles's,' ' Tales from Chaucer,'
' St John preaching in the Wilderness,' and
a large family picture of fourteen figures—
my father at the pianoforte, surrounded
by his wife and children and one or two
musical friends. Some dainty water-colour
pictures he also produced — four poetical
representations of ' The Four Seasons,' and
a lovely one of ' Christ near His Tomb,
seen by Mary Magdalene, who takes Him
for the Gardener,' besides many others in
the same style. The copies Edward made
of celebrated pictures are numerous ; among

them are Rubens's 'Triumph of Silenus,' Titian's 'Entombment of Christ,' Raphael's 'Head of a Friend,' Vandyke's 'Head of the Young Duke of Buckingham,' etc., etc. All these paintings, amounting to more than a hundred, by one who was still in his youth, for we lost him a few months ere he attained his twenty-third birthday.

While we were at Cambridge we were introduced to some of its Fellows, and we enjoyed many delicious wanderings in the gardens belonging to the different colleges. In one of them Charles took his hat off beneath the tree said to have been planted by Milton. In another we stood and gazed many times, admiring the beautiful architecture of St John's Chapel, and lingered listening to the 'murmur of innumerable bees' above our heads among the tall lime trees of the noble avenue. In these gardens we had a rather amusing incident. We had taken a basket containing some almond cakes to crunch while we sat to rest, but when

we quitted the gardens we had forgotten
our intention and left the basket and its
contents on one of the seats. One of the
Fellows, finding this supply of goodies,
disposed of them on the spot, but hearing afterwards who were their owners
and that we were leaving Cambridge, he
sent us a basket of similar cakes, inscribed
with the words, 'Viaticum for the journey.'
He was a very agreeable gentleman, and
for some time after kept up the acquaintance he had made with us at Cambridge.
During our stay in that noble place of
learning, I was so fortunate as to hear
a Greek oration delivered by one of the
students there. The sonorous beauty of
the language gratified my ear with a
lasting recollection of its rich sound.
My husband availed himself of the advantage gained from this visit, by writing
two letters on the Fitzwilliam Museum
at Cambridge for the 'Atlas' newspaper, and in the autumn of that
year, Leigh Hunt's 'Tatler' having been

started, Charles was engaged to write several of its theatrical and operatic notices, when its editor was occasionally otherwise employed in literary work. We were still living in Frith Street, when a few weeks of anxiety came to me. My husband was not quite well, and grew so weak that when we went for change of air to our dear old Enfield, he—so stout a walker and so swift a runner— had to take my arm once as we slowly ascended Windmill Hill together. Enfield air not effecting the cure we had hoped, we returned to town ; and there my mother prescribed a daily mutton chop and a glass of port wine at noon. The mutton chop I took pleasure and pride in cooking myself, and I think I may venture to affirm that never was mutton chop better broiled. Certain it is that this strengthening *régime* brought the much-desired cure. We continued to practise the strict economy we had early agreed to observe ; and, among other

savings of expense, I made all the clothes
I wore, as well as my husband's dress
waistcoats. One of these I especially remember for it was embroidered by my
mother, on black satin, with a wreath of
ivy leaves and berries in their natural
colours as its border. I mention these
particulars in order to show that a woman
who adopts literary work as her profession
need not either neglect or be deficient in
the more usually feminine accomplishments
of cookery and needlework.

We spent very happy days at this
juncture. My father had the joy of seeing his sons and daughters beginning their
several appointed pursuits in life prosper-
ously, and of having them in his own
home give evidence of the musical talent
they inherited from him, and the pro-
ficiency they had severally attained therein.
Among his younger daughters he had
soprano voices, and his eldest daughter supplied him with a meek counter tenor. His
sons Alfred and Edward had each a bass

voice, and his son-in-law, Charles, sang
tenor. No day passed without my father's
own canon 4 in 2, 'Give thanks to God,'
being sung as a grace after dinner; and
no first of May was allowed to pass without my husband's song, 'Old May Morning,' set to music by my father, being invariably sung by us to him. We had not
yet left Frith Street when a most memorable musical evening took place there. It
was just after Malibran's marriage with
De Beriot, and they both came to a
party at our house. De Beriot played
in a string quartette by Haydn, his tone
being one of the loveliest I ever heard
on the violin — not excepting that of
Paganini, who certainly was a marvellous
executant. Then Malibran gave, in generously lavish succession, Mozart's 'Non più
di fiori,' with Willman's obligato accompaniment on the Corno di bassetto; a 'Sancta
Maria' of her host's composition (which
she sang at sight with consummate effect
and expression), a tenderly graceful air,

'Ah, rien n'est doux comme la voix qui dit je t'aime,' and lastly a spirited mariner's song, with a sailorly burden, chiming with their rope hauling. In these two latter she accompanied herself; and when she had concluded, amid a rave of admiring plaudits from all present, she ran up to one of the heartiest among the applauding guests — Felix Mendelssohn —and said, in her own winning, playfully imperious manner (which a touch of foreign speech and accent made only the more fascinating),—'Now, Mr Mendelssohn, I never do nothing for nothing; you must play for me now I have sung for you.' He, 'nothing loath,' let her lead him to the pianoforte, where he dashed into a wonderfully impulsive extempore — masterly, musician - like, full of gusto. In this marvellous improvisation he introduced the several pieces Malibran had just sung, working them with admirable skill one after the other, and finally in combination, the four subjects blended together

in elaborate counter-point. When Mendelssohn had finished playing, my father
turned to a friend near him and said,—
'He has done some things that seem
to me to be impossible, even after I
have heard them done.' A strong proof
was given of the effect Mendelssohn had
produced upon the musical soul of the
host of the evening by his writing, the
very next morning, the canon just alluded
to, which the composer entitled 'A Thanks-
giving after Enjoyment.' The visit
Mendelssohn was then paying to England
was the first season of a German operatic
company's performance in London, at the
Italian Opera House, in the Haymarket,
and the morning after it had given
Beethoven's 'Fidelio,' with Haitzinger as
Florestan, and Schroeder Devrient as
Leonora, Mendelssohn called upon my
father, and sitting near the pianoforte,
turned every few minutes to the instrument, playing favourite 'bits' from the
opera of overnight. My father was so

enchanted with this young musician's genius, that one of his friends said to him,—' Novello, you'll spoil that young man.' The reply was—' He's too genuinely good to be spoiled.' I had the privilege of being taken by my father to hear Felix Mendelssohn play on the St Paul's organ, and a masterful piece of pedal-playing it was. The last time I heard him in England was at a concert of the Philharmonic Society, when he played Bach's fugue on his own name. At one of the Düsseldorf festivals, I had the privilege of meeting Mendelssohn a good deal. He conducted his own fine psalm, ' As the Hart pants,' played some of his own compositions ; and I even had the rare privilege of hearing him sing, at a morning rehearsal, when he wanted to give the artist who was to sing the song in the evening a precise idea of how he wished a particular passage to be rendered. His voice was small— like that of many composers—but capable of most musician-like expression. He was very companionable and easy in manner. Once he and I had a quiet talk together, he leaning on the back of a chair and asking news of the London Philharmonic Society, while, on another morning, he invited us (my mother and Clara, with whom I was at that time in Düsseldorf for a holiday on the Rhine) to go with him to the public gardens and taste some *Maitrank*, as we had not already made acquaintance with that famous Rhenish beverage. He was much amused at our saying it was 'nice, innocent stuff,' and warned us not to imagine it 'too innocent.'

Another delightful musician who, while he was in London, came to see my father, was Hummel. He, like Mendelssohn, was great in improvisation. So symmetrical, correct and mature in construction was it, that, as my father's musical friend, Charles Stokes, observed, 'You might count the time to every bar he played while improvising.'

Early in 1834 my father removed from

Frith Street to 69 Dean Street, his son
Alfred's music-selling business having so
much increased as to require larger premises.
It was the year of the Westminster Abbey
festival. My father was engaged to preside
at the organ, and his daughter Clara, Miss
Stephens and other vocalists were the singers
on this notable occasion. I remember hearing Miss Stephens saying, just before she
entered the choir to sing 'I know that my
Redeemer liveth,' 'Any young girl I knew,
however great her excellence in singing
might be, I would never advise to enter
the profession if she suffered from nervousness. I have never got over that which I
feel when I have to sing before the public.'
She had then been an established favourite
for years, and was especially famed for
singing ballads exquisitely. Her 'Auld
Robin Gray' was noted for its pathos and
beauty. The remark she made at the
Abbey was elicited by Clara's enviable
calmness and absence of anything like
trepidation while singing the lovely air

allotted to her, 'How beautiful are the feet.' That quiet truthfulness, that pure, firm, silvery voice precisely suited the devout words. And as regards Clara's subsequent singing of the very song Miss Stephens had then to sing, it was remarkable for the pious fervour of its pouring forth. Clara said that she always felt, while singing 'I know that my Redeemer liveth,' that she was performing an act of faith. When she was at the Court of Berlin, some years afterwards, his Prussian Majesty always asked her to repeat to him that particular song each time she went to the palace.

It was while we were living at Dean Street that my sister Cecilia's marriage took place. She had already made a good musical career; for she—like us all —had begun early an active entrance upon industrial life. She had sung in various musical pieces at London theatres, and had pleased greatly as an opera-singer for two seasons at Edinburgh. She married

Mr Serle, author of several dramas and two romances, besides being editor for some years of a London newspaper. At Cecilia's wedding - breakfast we first made acquaintance with that fine wit—dear Douglas Jerrold. Hardly a greater mistake could be made than to attribute bitterness or ill-nature to Douglas Jerrold's sharpest sarcasms, as sometimes was the case by those who merely heard of them and did not know his real nature. We, who did know him, understood them better. He was deeply earnest in all serious things, and very much in earnest when dealing with less apparently important matters, which he thought needed the scourge of a sarcasm. His concern for the object of his satirical quips was often at the root of them ; and he would pour forth his keen flights of pointed arrows chiefly with the view of rousing to improvement his butt, whom he knew capable of better things, and on whom the shafts of his ridicule might tell to

good purpose rather than harm. This
was the origin of many of the sharp
things he said against woman ; for instance, such as those he wrote in ' The
Man made of Money,' ' Mrs Caudle's
Lectures,' etc. He reserved to himself
the right to snub the Mrs Jerichos and
the Mrs Caudles among the sex, to rebuke
their shrewish use of tongue, their hen-
peckings, their unworthy wheedling and
meannesses ; but he had faith in the
innate worth of womanhood, and its
superiority to such basenesses, where it
trusts its own honest nature and disdains
resorting to such degrading tricks of
hectoring or coaxing. Of woman's
generous unselfishness and quiet heroism
Jerrold had full perception, as we had
many opportunities of noticing, in some
of the side remarks he occasionally let
fall in conversation with us.

As a token of his belief that he was entirely
understood and appreciated by my Charles
and me, I may mention that when he brought

his 'Mrs Caudle's Lectures' as a presenta-
tion copy to me, he had written in its blank
page,—'Presented with great timidity, but
equal regard, to Mrs Cowden-Clarke, by
Douglas Jerrold.' His promptitude as well
as stinging power in retort is well known;
the words that excited his reprisals had
scarcely issued from the mouth of him who
spoke them, when out sprang Jerrold's reply.
The celebrated one to the man who said,
'Ah, Lamartine and I row in the same
boat,' was met by the answer, 'Not with
the same *scull*, though,' without a second's
pause.

Many a charmingly witty letter did we
receive from Douglas Jerrold; many a delightful hour of talk did we enjoy with
him; and he became a dear and admired
friend of ours.

'Poor and content is rich and rich enough,'
truly and wisely says our beloved Shakespeare; certain it is that my husband and
I verified to the utmost these words. We
were happiest of the happy, not only while

practising strictest economy, but in avail-
ing ourselves of every literary or artistic
means for gaining addition to our scanty
income. One of these means presented itself in an engagement to sing in the services of Somers Town chapel, where my
brother Alfred sang bass and led the choir.
This engagement was the means of our
hearing Cardinal Wiseman preach a beautiful and learned sermon upon altar-pieces,
one of them having been a recent donation
to that chapel. His learning—great as it
was—always seemed to be ready stored at
his command, but never allowed to be
brought out ostentatiously. We had the great
pleasure of hearing him deliver a lecture
at the Marylebone Institution, on the influence of words at various epochs of
'civilisation in the world.' He showed how
far superior, in impressive effect, were such
simple words as 'graveyard,' 'God's acre,'
to the more classically - derived names
—'Necropolis,' or 'cemetery;' or such an
expression as 'child-murder' to 'infanticide.'

I shall not easily forget the manner in which
he discussed the absolute necessity of keeping one's temper as the best, nay only,
means of obtaining and preserving 'power.'
He seemed to rise several inches as he
drew up his person to its full height in
pronouncing that single word. He was of
rotund proportions, and he used to relate
with great gusto the circumstance that when
he was staying at Lord Clifford's house,
Ugbrook Park, one of the maid-servants
there, who had been told that his proper
title was 'your Eminence,' used to say, as
she dropped her reverential curtsey, 'Yes,
your Immense.' This same damsel—who
evidently possessed no accurate ear—when
twelve Jesuits were on a visit to Ugbrook,
said, 'There's a matter of a dozen Jezebels
come here.' Cardinal Wiseman's lecture on
'William Shakespeare' is one of the very
best commentaries on our greatest poet that
I know. It was printed and published in
1865, after its author's decease; but the
preface states that the Cardinal would have

desired 'it should be given to the people of England as the last work he undertook for their sake.'

Another source of gaining increase of pelf arose out of Charles's gift in reading aloud untiringly, together with his possessing a speaking voice so full, so flexible, so varied in expression and intonation, that it was peculiarly fitted for addressing a large audience. These natural advantages suggested to me the idea that he would succeed capitally as a lecturer ; and on telling him this, we talked the matter over together (according to his wonted habit of consulting his wife on all projects), and he not only adopted the idea, but set to work at once in selecting subjects from among his favourite poetic authors, and in forming plans for obtaining engagements to deliver his lectures when written. The complete success that crowned this undertaking cannot be better manifested than by quoting from what his friend, the enthusiastic Shakespearian, Mr Sam Timmins,

wrote when requested to give a record of
Charles Cowden-Clarke's career as lecturer.
The following is the passage to which I
allude :—' He began the great work of his
life—the public lectures on Shakespeare and
other dramatists and poets—which made his
name throughout Great Britain, and secured
him crowded and delighted audiences. His
lecturing career commenced at a period
when mechanics' institutions were waning
in interest, and a demand was growing
for lectures of a more literary and attractive character than merely scientific lectures,
even with many experiments and demon-
strations, could supply. The lecture-room
was just beginning to be the school-house
of the middle classes, whose education had
been imperfect, but who had acquired the
desire to learn more. Such a demand
Cowden-Clarke was especially qualified to
supply, and his lectures soon became the
great attraction at "Atheneum," and "In-
stitute," and "Lecture-hall" all through the
land. His lectures were really "lectures,"

read from MS. most carefully prepared
and splendidly and clearly written in the
old style "round hand" which Lamb admired. They were not, however, merely
" read," but every word was given with
such earnestness and force that every
hearer caught the enthusiasm of the
lecturer, and was led to go home and
read more.

'As a lecturer, Cowden-Clarke had very
special qualifications. He had a pleasant,
cheerful, ruddy face, a charming humour
of expression, a clear, pleasant voice, and
a heartiness and drollness of manner which
won the audience as soon as he appeared.
His were careful essays, the result of long
and patient study, full of acute and subtle
criticism, and always throwing new lights
on the subject in hand. The expectations
of his audience were aroused, and they
were never disappointed. His good taste
secured audiences who never entered a
theatre, and to whom the drama generally
was a sealed book. He lectured on Shake-

speare—his fools, his clowns, his kings, on special characters or plays; and every library soon found an increased demand for Shakespeare's works, and new editions were soon forthcoming. It is no exaggeration to say that very much of the increased interest in Shakespeare among English readers is to be traced to the lectures of Cowden - Clarke. One of his hearers once hit the secret of his success. "You like what you are talking about, and therefore you make your hearers like it too." Throughout Great Britain he was ever welcome, and his loss as a lecturer was never fully made up, for he combined so many attractions of subject, style, treatment, personation and humour as are very rarely found united in one person. While his analysis of dramatic characters was masterly and searching, and his touches of pathos delicately suggestive, the full force of his delineations came out in his representation of comic characters from Shakespeare and Molière especially. He

was not a mere rhetorician, elocutionist or
actor.   He never attempted to personate
the characters, but only to read with such
interest and power as to realise the very
"form and fashion" of each. He was, in
fact, as dramatically successful as a "reader"
of the highest class as Dickens when reading his own stories ; and Cowden-Clarke's
range was wider and his characters more
varied.'

Charles's first-delivered lecture   ('On
Chaucer') was at Royston in 1835, and he
at once achieved success ; receiving such un-
animous plaudits and testimonies of admiration not only from his audience, but from
several residents in the town, who, hearing the
impression he had produced, invited him to
their houses and became permanent friends.
This was the case in many places where he
subsequently lectured ; men of distinguished
talent and eminence forming lifelong friend-
ships with him.   At first, when he lectured
at provincial institutions, he took me with
him ; but finding this naturally diminished

our profits, we agreed to forego this pleasure
by limiting it to my accompanying him to
the railway station when he left, and meeting
him there when he returned home. Our
daily interchange of letters made the best
compensation for absence from each other ;
and he never failed in sending me one—sometimes two—daily. His handwriting was a
nobly clear one. He preferred reading his
lectures from his own MS. even to reading
them from print, when some of them, in after
years, appeared in book form. When he was
in London he kept brother Alfred's ledgers
and day-books posted up, and he made fair
copies of almost everything that he or I wrote
for publication. In order to ensure perfectly
effective delivery when lecturing, he invariably
rehearsed the lecture to be given in the evening by reading it aloud that same morning.
When he was in town, he read it to me ; when
away from town, he read it aloud to himself,
so unsparing of pains was he in everything
he undertook. While thus engaged in his
lecturing and book-keeping, Charles still

maintained his other writing in literary work.
He wrote 'The Musician about Town,' and
a lovely tale called 'Gentleness is Power,' or
the story of 'Caranza and Aborzuf' for the
'Analyst Magazine.' He was almost an exceptional husband in his generous mode of
making the masculine prerogative of complete
marital sway cede to his idea of the right and
happiness of conjugal equality. He brought
every guinea he earned to me to take care of,
and whenever I consulted him on any needful
purchase, his answer always was :—'It is as
much your money as mine, do what you
think well with it ; buy what you think proper,
and what we can best afford.' After some
time of our living in Dean Street, my father
removed to Bayswater, where we first in-
habited No. 4 Craven Hill, and subsequently
No. 9, which was called 'Craven Hill
Cottage.' These houses were pleasantly
simple, and had a field, skirted by a row
of fine tall trees, in front of them ; trees,
alas ! ruthlessly hewn down, when so-called
'improvements' in later years were com-

menced. Both our Craven Hill homesteads
had small gardens behind them, beyond which
gardens was still another field. But I have
learned that the whole of this pretty locality
has given place to modernly built ranges of
tall edifices, fashionable houses, and 'desirable
residences.' When we removed to Bayswater,
Alfred still went up to business at 69 Dean
Street ; and my sister Sabilla organised a singing class there for young ladies, to which she
and I went on the appointed days each week.
My father, with his wonted assiduity wherever music was concerned, invariably used to
hear me go through the pieces that were to
be performed every morning before I went
up to town with my sister, who wished me
to join those of her pupils who had counter
tenor voices. Sabilla's artistic career was a
congenial one. She was a favourite concert-
singer for some years ; she made her *début*
on the stage in Rossini's 'La Gazza ladra' ;
she sang his 'Semiramide' and other prima-
donna parts in Dublin ; she was an admirable teacher of vocalisation, and wrote an

excellent treatise on 'Voice and Vocal Art.'
My father had the delight of seeing his
children succeed in all the professional careers
they themselves had respectively chosen, and
our life at Bayswater was a very cheerful and
interesting one. We had for neighbours
there two that were especially productive
of pleasure to us. Mrs Loudon and her
daughter Agnes occupied one house in
Porchester Terrace, while the Reverend Mr
Tagart and his family resided at another in
the same road, which was close to Craven
Hill—so close, that a hood and shawl over
my dress sufficed me for going to visit at
either house. At Mrs Loudon's we met the
Landseers—Edwin and Charles ; Martin, the
painter of 'Belshazzar's Feast,' etc. ; his
clever-headed and amiable daughter, Miss
Martin ; Joseph Bonomi and his wife, who
was another daughter of Martin ; Owen Jones ;
Noel Humphreys ; Samuel Lover, author of
that sprightly novel, 'Rory O'More' ; William
Jerdan and others. Of Edwin Landseer we
heard the amusing incident of his having been

at the English Court when the King of
Portugal was on a visit to our Queen, and the
celebrated painter of animals being presented
to him, his Portuguese Majesty graciously
said :—'I am very glad to see you, Mr
Landseer, for I am *very* fond of beasts.'
We also heard of Edwin Landseer's wonderful feat when someone was talking of being
able to write or draw with the left hand, and
he remarked :—'I think I can not only draw
with my left hand, but I can draw with both
hands at once.' Whereupon he took up two
pencils and actually drew a horse with one
hand and a dog with the other, at the same
time.

At the Reverend Mr Tagart's house we met
serene-spirited Emerson and other noted
Americans ; and one morning Mrs Tagart
sent round a message telling me that, if
Charles and I would go and lunch with her,
she expected Mrs Gaskell to come and see
her then, knowing how glad we should be to
meet the authoress of ' Mary Barton ' (a book
that Charles Dickens had written his thanks

for, and admiration of, to Mrs Gaskell herself). It was just like Mrs Tagart's thoughtful
kindness to send us this welcome invitation. The lady guest proved to be a remarkably quiet-mannered woman ; thoroughly
unaffected, thoroughly attractive ; so modest
that she blushed like a girl when we hazarded
some expression of our ardent admiration
of her ' Mary Barton.' So full of enthusiasm
on general subjects of humanity and benevol-
ence that she talked freely and animatedly
at once upon them with us ; and so young in
appearance and manner that we could hardly
believe her to be the mother of two daughters
she mentioned in terms that showed them to
be no longer children.

It was while we were living at Craven
Hill that I finished my ' Concordance to
Shakespeare,' writing the last line of the
work on my dear mother's birthday, the
17th of August 1841. When, later on, it
was published, the correction of the proofs
and seeing it through the Press occupied a
considerable time of additional labour. I

there wrote my 'Kit Bam's Adventures', and my novel of 'The Iron Cousin'; but before these two books were published, we took a most delightful holiday journey to Italy in 1847. We had but a month to spare from our several avocations, but on consultation together we resolved to make the sacrifice; for, as my brother Alfred truly observed, 'If we had no engagements to give up, we should be so badly off as to be without any.' Accordingly, he gave up some of his, my Charles some of his, and my sister Sabilla some of hers; but thoroughly we enjoyed our trip with our dear parents. From Ramsgate to Ostend, through Germany, by the Rhine, to Switzerland, by the Lake of Lucerne to that of Como, on to Milan, Verona and Venice, where we spent an enchanting few days ere we took our way back to England. We had brought with us the four green-bound books in which my father had collected and arranged for us two hundred and five of the choicest compositions, such as Mozart's

'Ave Verum,' Leonardo Leo's 'Kyrie eleison,' Wilbye's 'Flora gave me,' Linley's 'Let me careless,' etc., etc. These unaccompanied concerted pieces my father entitled 'Music for the open air,' and they enabled us to give him the enjoyment of his favourite gratification whenever he and we spent a day in the fields or took a journey. In Venice they were specially welcome companions, for they accompanied us whenever we were in our gondola, gliding about seeing the most remarkable spots in that uniquely beautiful city of the sea; and then, on reaching the most retired and quiet of the lagoons, indulging in a family quartett. When our gondolier, Antonio, perceived this, he generally chose one of the less-frequented water streets, and we once overheard him say to one of his fellow - gondoliers, — 'My English people often sing, I can tell you, and well, too!'

On our return home we found that Mrs Loudon was getting up, for performance at her house, Sheridan's play of 'The Rivals.'

Her daughter was to play Lydia Languish, while Alfred, Sabilla and I had been 'cast' for three of the characters—nay, four, for my brother was to double the parts of the Coachman and David, while Sabilla was to play Lucy, and I was to enact Mrs Malaprop. Other friends of Mrs Loudon sustained the rest of the characters, and the performance, which took place the 10th November 1847, was completely successful—so successful, indeed, that it had to be repeated next evening, and again on the 12th of the ensuing January 1848.

These private theatricals led to one of the most peculiarly bright episodes of my life. At a party at Mrs Tagart's house I was introduced by Leigh Hunt to Charles Dickens, with whom we had been for some time acquainted through his delightful books, and he had been always spoken of in our family circle as 'dear Dickens' or 'darling Dickens'; therefore it may easily be conceived how pleased and proud I felt to be thus personally made known to him. He

and I fell at once into liveliest conversation ;
and just before he was taking leave, he
said, 'I hear you have been playing Mrs
Malaprop lately.'   I answered, 'Yes ; and
I hear you are going to get up an amateur
performance of the " Merry Wives," so I
could be your Dame Quickly.'   I saw that
he did not take this seriously ; accordingly,
I wrote to him, a day or two after, telling
him I was in earnest when I had made the
offer to act Dame Quickly, if he cared to
let me do so.

The note I received in reply began with
a sentence that threw me into a rapture of
excitement and delight.   The sentence was
as follows :—

'DEAR MRS COWDEN-CLARKE,—I did
not understand, when I had the pleasure of
conversing with you the other evening, that
you had really considered the subject and
desired to play.   But I am very glad to
understand it now, and I am sure there will
be a universal sense among us of the grace

Charles Cowden Clarke
Mary
2161

and appropriateness of such a proceeding.
. . . Will you receive this as a solemn
" call " to " rehearsal" of " The Merry Wives "
at Miss Kelly's theatre to-morrow, Saturday
week, at seven in the evening ? '

Although I am naturally shy, I have never
felt shy when acting, but it must be confessed
that ' rehearsal' was somewhat of a heart-
beating affair to me as I had to meet and
speak before such a group of distinguished
men as John Forster, editor of the ' Examiner;'
Mark Lemon, editor of 'Punch ; ' John
Leech, its inimitable illustrator ; the admirable artists, Augustus Egg and Frank Stone,
all of whom were fellow-actors in Charles
Dickens's Amateur Company. But he, as
manager, presenting me to them with his
usual grace and kindliness, together with
my own firm resolve to speak out clearly,
just as if I were at performance instead of
rehearsal, helped me capitally through this
first and most formidable evening. On the
night when ' The Merry Wives ' was first

I

performed at the Haymarket Theatre (15th of May 1848), I felt not a shadow of that stage fright, although I had to make my entrance before a select London audience. As I stood at the side-scene with Augustus Egg (who played Simple, Master Slender's man-servant), waiting to go on together, he asked me whether I felt nervous. 'Not in the least,' I replied. 'What I feel is joyful excitement, not alarm.' Augustus Egg's artist eye remarked the appropriateness of my costume, and added, 'It looks not so *new* as those made by the theatrical robe-makers, but as if it had been worn in the streets of Windsor day by day.' I answered, 'Well it may, for I made it myself, and with material already part of my own wear.' I had had the advantage of Colonel Hamilton's obliging suggestions and sketches, as well as hints I took from Kenny Meadows' picture of Dame Quickly in the 'Illustrated Shakespeare,' published by Tyas in 1843.

The performance of 'The Merry Wives'

J. ALFRED NOVELLO.

at the Haymarket Theatre was followed by
that of Ben Jonson's 'Every Man in His
Humour,' and Kenny's farce of 'Love, Law
and Physic' on the next evening but one
(17th May 1848). In the former I played
Tib, Cob's wife; and in the latter, Mrs
Hillary; and for both these characters I
made my own dresses. In one of her
concluding scenes, when Mrs Hillary pre-
tends to be a rich Spanish lady, and tries
to obtain a proposal of marriage from
Lubin Log, I made a sparkling addition
to the velvet dress I donned, by orna-
menting it with a set of stage-diamond
buttons, which had belonged to Elliston,
had been bought by my sister Cecilia, and
was kindly lent by her to me for this
purpose. Besides these large buttons,
farther effect was produced by a brilliant
tiara of the same stage-gems, with which
I fastened the high Spanish comb and
veil I wore; and Mark Lemon, who enacted Lubin Log admirably, used to make
a point of kissing his hand to these

diamonds, showing what was his chief attraction in wooing this supposed heiress to millions. Charles Dickens, supreme as manager, super-excellent as actor, and ardently enthusiastic in his enjoyment of exercising his skill in both capacities, organised a series of provincial engagements for the performance of his amateur company. At Manchester, on the 3d June 1848, we played 'The Merry Wives' and 'Animal Magnetism'; at Liverpool, on the 5th June 1848, 'Merry Wives' and 'Love, Law and Physic'; at Birmingham, on 6th June, 'Every Man in His Humour' and 'Animal Magnetism.' At Birmingham again, on the 27th June 1848, 'Merry Wives,' 'Love, Law and Physic,' and 'Two o'clock in the Morning'; at Edinburgh, on the 17th July 1848, 'Merry Wives' 'Love, Law and Physic,' and 'Two o'clock in the Morning'; at Glasgow, on 18th July 1848, 'Merry Wives' and 'Animal Magnetism'; and at Glasgow, on the 20th July 1848, we gave 'Used up,' 'Love,

Law and Physic,' and 'Two o'clock in the
Morning.' It was our last performance
together, and we not only felt regret at the
time for this close of our happy comrade-
ship, but dear Charles Dickens's letters for a
long time afterwards expressed his pain at its
cessation. Genial, kind, most sympathetic and
fascinating was his companionship, and very
precious to me was his friendship.

In the autumn of that year my dear
mother's health became so delicate that our
medical adviser counselled her removal to a
warmer climate ; and she chose Nice (then
Italian) for the proposed purpose. My sister
Sabilla gave up all her pursuits in England
and accompanied her abroad ; and they took
up their abode in a pleasant set of apartments
in a house that had a garden stretching down
to the seashore, and was so truly southern
that it had rose hedges taller than the height
of a man, besides having abundance of orange
trees skirting its paths. The next year, Alfred, Charles and I (with my father, who remained at Nice) took a journey, to spend some

weeks with my mother and Sabilla, during
the long vacation, when my brother could
be best spared from his business, and a delightful time we had.

On our return to Bayswater we three began
what we called our ' trihominate ' homestead ;
and we tried to make it as cheerful and happy
as we could, lessened as it now was by the
absence of our dear ones. Weekly interchange of long, closely-written letters between
my mother and me kept us mentally together,
in their minute details of what took place
daily at each home. We were interested in
her improved health and daily drives in the
Nice picturesque environs or walks in the
Nice garden : while she followed all our dis-
posals of time in England. They were mostly
thus : My dear men-folk went up to the
Dean Street music warehouse every morning
after breakfast ; I attended to our household
arrangements, and worked away at my writing
(' The Girlhood of Shakespeare's Heroines,'
etc.) during the day, and then had the joy of
walking to meet my men-folk on their way

home to dinner, generally taking the path
which led through Kensington Gardens and
Hyde Park as our line for meeting. We
resolved to take advantage of the long vacation each year for a journey to Nice, when I
used to take the MSS. of those books I had in
hand with me, that I might have the pleasure
of reading them to my mother, and consulting with her as to her opinion and judgment
respecting them. In her drives and walks she
always made me her companion until the time
arrived for our return to England. On one
of these Nice visits of ours we saw Clara for
the first time after she was married to Count
Gigliucci on the 22d November (St Cecilia's
day) 1843, as they had always since their
marriage dwelt in his patrimonial mansion at
Fermo on the shores of the Adriatic. But at
this juncture they had come to Nice for a
change, and were contemplating Clara's re-
sumption of her artistic career. We also
then made acquaintance with her four children
—two sons and two daughters—who, I must
say, were the most adorable human cherubs I

ever beheld. My readers may believe me, and would believe me, could they have seen them, with their fair complexions and floppy golden curls, dancing about in their grand-mamma's garden.

We were preparing for our yearly visit to Nice in 1854 when a telegram reached us to let us know that our beloved mother had sunk into eternal rest on the 25th July. Of our misery at this irreparable loss I say nothing, even if I could find words to give it expression.

In 1856 my brother Alfred resolved to retire from business, which he made over to his faithful and able manager, Mr Henry Littleton, who had been for many years known to him as an excellent aid and seconder in all his views. The name of ' Novello & Company ' was still retained ; and its present form of ' Novello, Ewer & Company ' adopted at a later date.

Nice was selected as the spot which the ' trihominate ' preferred, for the sake of its climate and for the sake of its associations ; also because my father, my sister Sabilla, and

the young Gigliuccis were dwelling there.
These latter became our chief source of
brightness, and producer of the cheerfulness
we strove earnestly to maintain. The boys,
Giovanni and Mario, had been placed by
their parents in college, while the two little
girls, Porzia and Valeria, were established
(under the care of a worthy couple, friends
of the Count) in a house near to ours, *Maison
Quaglia.*

Charles made it a pleasure to give Clara's
little girls lessons in writing, and in correct
reading of, as well as learning by heart, English verse ; while to see him with one of them
on his knee, repeating her 'Gay's Fables,'
fondling his silver hair, and calling him
her 'dearest boy,' filled my heart with happy
feeling. Invariably these lessons were at a
table on which stood a case of English barley-
sugar, imported expressly, and from it Porzia
and Valeria were permitted to help themselves
at the conclusion of their so-called 'tasks,'
these being rather play work than task work.
From then to the present time these two

darlings have been as dear to me as if they were my own children.

Time passed smoothly on during our residence at Nice. Charles and I steadily pursued our literary work, he bringing out his 'Riches of Chaucer,' and his 'Carmina Minima,' besides editing the text of Nichol's 'Library Edition of the British Poets,' while I was engaged by the Messrs Appleton of New York to write 'World-noted Women,' and to edit their edition of Shakespeare. This last work was the source of peculiar pride and gratification to my husband and me, inasmuch as it made me the first (and as yet, only) woman editor of our great poet. We took daily walks together, and more than once got up before dawn to see the sun rise, and Charles continued a favourite practice of his in reading a bit from some favourite author to me before we all met at our first meal.

Although his public delivery of lectures had ceased on his leaving England, yet my husband frequently read one of them to our friends in our Nice parlour, and he never relinquished a time - honoured custom he had of reading one to us while we stoned raisins, blanched almonds, cut candied fruit, etc., for the Christmas pudding, which we continued to make yearly in honour of dear old England.

Count Gigliucci and his wife, our Clara, used to flit over to Nice whenever they could get away from her renewed engagements, in order to see their children ; and this brought us delightful music, as well as was the cause of a great treat, when Tamburini came one afternoon to our house and sang with Clara several delicious operatic duets. He kept wonderfully young and alert, and was very gay and bright in society. He laughed playfully, I recollect, at my having taken part in a Mendelssohn Trio, wherein Clara and her daughter, Porzia, sang the two soprano parts, my counter-tenor being correct, but very mild in tone, as usual. Both Clara's daughters, although such mere youngsters still, were already musically gifted, and at six o'clock one morning (my birthday) Charles and I were awakened by hearing Clara, Porzia and Valeria sing, under our window, Mendelssohn's charming trio, 'Hearts feel that love thee.'

Cecilia's daughter Mary, my god-daughter, having been sent to school at Nice while we were there, Sabilla got up a charming series of concerts for the three girls—Mary, Porzia and Valeria—for which they were to make out the programmes themselves and sing the pieces appointed for each performance.

More than one distinguished person were visitors of ours while we were at Nice, among others Mr Francis Child, an ardent Chaucerian then, and Professor at Harvard College, Cambridge, America, since. He is author of a poem called 'The Child of Bristowe,' written in delightfully antique style and true to Chaucer's manner, which he sent to us some years afterwards. A friend of his—who also became one of

ours—was likewise at Nice when he was
there. This was Mrs John Farrar,
authoress of 'Advice to Young Ladies,' and
'Recollections of Seventy Years.' She was
most energetically kind and serviceable to
sufferers during the American war between
North and South, and as clever as she
was good.

An illustrious visitor gratified us by
staying at our house for a few days—no
other than Richard Cobden, who had been
known to my brother Alfred in England
at the time of the 'Anti-Corn Law League.'
Easy, familiarly at home with us, he used
to read his English newspapers aloud to
us or chat with us as if he had been one
of our family circle for years, and when
on one Christmas Eve we made our
traditional plum-pudding (Mrs Cobden helping us to prepare its ingredients), he kept
up entertaining conversation the while. Next
day, when the pudding was to be eaten, and
he with my brother and sister were engaged
to discuss its merits at a neighbouring friend's

house, Cobden looked up at Charles and me (who were standing on the terrace steps remaining at home to keep house) and expressed his hearty regret that we should not be of the party to enjoy this truly British 'consecrated cate.'

When Nice became under French rule, we found many of its ways so much changed that we resolved to leave it for an Italian residence, and fixing upon Genoa as a proved excellent climate, Alfred took Charles and me with him to see if we could find a suitable house there. We went over one (very near to that we have since dwelt in for more than thirty years) which was so curious that a description of it and our journey to and from Genoa on that occasion was written by me in a paper entitled 'The Cornice Road in Rain (though altered by the editor of the 'Atlantic Monthly Magazine' to, I think, the less individually appropriate name of 'An Italian Rainstorm'), because my kind friend, James T. Fields, had requested me to contribute an article to that magazine.

Before that year (1860) was ended, Alfred and Sabilla went again to Genoa to renew his search for a domicile that we should all like, and when he returned home to Nice he told us that he had bought the house and garden then called Pallazzo Massone, and subsequently named Villa Novello. On the eleventh of the following April, Alfred and Sabilla took possession of his new purchase, but Charles and I remained at Nice with my father until our villa should be put in order for his reception as there were many alterations needed to anglicise it and make it more comfortable to live in. Alas! that reception was destined never to be. During the spring and summer my dear father was better than he had been for some time before. He read my preface to 'World-noted Women,' and the one to my American edition of Shakespeare, saying of the latter, in his encouraging way,—'It does you great credit, my dear.' He resumed his reading of some of his favourite books, which previously he had not cared to do. He had all his life been a great admirer of Walter Scott's fine novels, and the one he last was reading ('The Fair Maid of Perth'), I found face downwards at the page where he had left off when he was taken ill. Throughout that illness I had the privilege of attending upon him night and day. Patient, gentle, affectionate, he blessed me in the tenderest terms, in words that have been to me a most precious bequest ever since. Without pain, but desirous of rest, he expired in the evening of 9th August 1861.

A fitting memorial was allowed by the Dean and Chapter of Westminster Abbey to be placed in the North Transept there, in the shape of a stained - glass window, its appropriate subject being a Saint Cecilia, the patron saint of music.

My brother Alfred fetched my Charles and me to Genoa from Nice, where my sister Sabilla, with her usual unselfish activity in helping us, stayed to take the trouble of collecting our most-prized belongings — pictures, books, etc., etc., and

Villa Novello. Genoa. 1874.

causing them to be safely conveyed to our new abode. Being perched on a promontorial cliff, more than a hundred feet above the sea, this villa commands a magnificent view of the harbour and bay of Genoa, beyond which trends the coast of the Riviera for sixty miles, half-way to Nice, affording sight of gorgeous sunsets, often increased in beauty by the crescent moon and visiting planets. The expanse of sky and sea, the grandeur of this western view, cannot be taken from us ; but, otherwise, we have been the victim—as we were at Craven Hill—of so - called 'improvements.' When we first came here there was a small grove of cypress trees, marking the spot where lay the remains of numerous persons who died from a visitation of cholera one season long before. In this small grove was annually sung a dirge, for the repose of the souls of those who lay beneath, by some priests from the neighbouring church of San Giacomo, at early dawn, and the sound of their

K

solemn chaunting rose softly and sooth-
ingly to our ears as we lay and listened in
the coming on of morning light.

Then came a time when a decree from
high quarters swept away the peaceful
cypresses, and substituted a battery of
heavy guns, with what Leigh Hunt calls
'the fool cannon's ever-gaping mouth,'
turned seaward. On the eastern side of
our cliff-demesne there were three miniature cemeteries—one dedicated to the Swiss
Protestants, one to the Hebrew, and one
to the members of the Greek Church—all
three united amicably, side by side, by a
wooded enclosure of cypresses and one
graceful cedar tree. Through this cluster
came goldenly the glories of sunrise, and
amid this shade more than one blackbird
and thrush built their nest, and in the
springtime a faithful nightingale (William
Morris's 'brown bird') would linger there
for a day or two on its way to the closer
shelter of the Pegli Woods; and every
April a pair of hoopooes would visit us from

Africa, abide a fortnight or three weeks,
familiarly pecking about the green slope
immediately beneath our windows, and only
taking refuge with slow flight, plunging
into the thicket of cypresses when startled
by chance from its grassy meal of insects.
The dark verdure of these cemetery trees
was enlivened, on our side of the enclosure
wall, by a lush overgrowth of roses, big-
nonias, westaria, etc., while up some of the
slender boles and boughs clambered the
snowy sprays of the rincas, and in autumn
the gorgeous crimson of the Virginia
creeper richly draped them. The loveliness
of these three cemeteries was ruthlessly
snatched away from us by the intrusion of
a 'new road,' that cut through our croquet-
ground, our vineyard, and our east garden,
that moreover led from nothing to nowhere,
and that had its principal portion dedicated
to drilling recruits of a morning when
practising their 'goose-step,' and of an
afternoon to a rabble of boys out of school,
who finish their education by stone-throwing

and general mischief. Then, to crown this disturbance of our peaceful residence, two large steam hammers, smoking and banging away from morning to evening, were erected beneath our windows, to drive piles into the sandy soil; on these was built an ugly and thoroughly useless circular terrace, overlooking the sea, bare of trees, exposed to rain, dust, wind and glare, but which the architect thereof declared, with effusive admiration of his own design, 'would serve for the inhabitants of Genoa to contemplate the horizon.' Fortunately for us, these devastations were accomplished below the level of our house, so that our sea views still remain visible.

But to return to the period when we first lived here. My earliest piece of writing, in our new house, was one I had much at heart. It was 'The Life and Labours of Vincent Novello,' for I earnestly wished there should exist a record of the immense amount of musical work which his indefatigable industry and devotion to music had achieved, together with the very numerous publications which he had brought out to supply the world of music with delight, and to advance the knowledge and practice of this enchanting art. My health had not been strong since his loss, and it was deemed advisable that I should have change of air and scene ; accordingly, Sabilla, Charles and I indulged ourselves with an excursion to see the Correggio pictures at Parma, and the Caracci pictures at Bologna. Alfred remained at home to superintend the masons employed about the house, and to look to the arrangement of our garden, which had been little better than a cabbage-ground before our advent. To give an idea of the task he had in hand—he projected, and after some considerable time effected, the making of a piece of road, by way of a carriage drive, between the entrance gate and our house door. He had to build up a supporting wall against the earth of our west walk ; he pulled down some ramshackle outhouses that formed part of the old edifice, and substituted a terrace, paved with Pompeian tiles, beneath our western windows, preserving opposite to them the only tree we found here, a graceful bay-laurel, which Alfred kindly called my tree, and subsequently trained up its bole, and among its central branches, a climbing red rose. Beyond the bay-laurel tree a grass plot, or moderate-sized lawn, with a small fountain, backed by a sculptured group of boys at play, surrounded by variegated canes, a group of magnolias, a cedrus deodara, a eucalyptus, and a wellingtonia— both of these trees not taller than an umbrella when he first had them planted, but now giants of fifty feet high.

In that same year we took a short spring flight to a neighbouring bathing-place called Acqua Santa, and in the summer a longer flight to Turin, Paris and London, where we saw again many dear old English friends, heard the Handel festival in the Crystal Palace, and were present at two of Charles Dickens's 'readings.' One was the 'Christmas Carol,' and the 'Trial from Pickwick,' the other was from 'Nicholas Nickleby,' 'Boots at the Holly-tree Inn,' and 'Mrs Gamp.'

In the autumn I saw for the first time Italy's grand tragic actress, Ristori, especially great, I thought, in 'Giuditta' and in 'Elisabetta Regina d'Inghilterra.' We had already made delighted acquaintance with two of the most excellent comic actors—Toselli and Pieri. Toselli we had first seen in Nice, where he played many capital characters in the Piedmontese dialect. His style was exquisitely peculiar in humour, and Charles was so enthusiastic in his applause, that we afterwards heard that Toselli had said, 'Whenever my *Inglese* is among the audience, I always play better than usual.'

It may be judged how prolonged was the work of putting our Genoese house into order, when I mention that it was only in November that our dining-room was completed, and we able to eat our first Christmas dinner therein. A certain Signor Boccardo was its clever decorator, and so excellent in all respects was his work, that its beautiful design and the stable colours he used have lasted well till now. The walls of our picture gallery were painted from architectural designs of Salisbury Cathedral, and our vestibule and staircase have frescoes copied from Raphael's 'Hours.' The walls of our music-room we found ornamented in the antique Genoese style of arabesque painting and relievo medallions. This ornamentation had been strangely covered over with whitewash by former occupants (!), but was restored by an Italian artist whom Alfred employed for the purpose.

The next year, 1863, is chiefly memorable to me from its being the one in which we were requested by Messrs Cassell & Company to edit their annotated edition of Shakespeare, and we began the work on the 1st of September. It was rather an anxious task, as

we had to 'work to time,' for the edition
was originally brought out in weekly numbers ; but we never failed once in regular
pre-supply of the requisite matter for the
printers. Besides his joint-editing with me,
Charles made a fair copy of the '14,533
Notes,' 'Shakespeare's Life,' Preface, etc.,
which we wrote for this work, as well as
of the one which followed it ; for immediately upon its completion, we began a
book that we had long contemplated—'The
Shakespeare Key.' We finished our annotated edition on the 16th March 1868,
and began our 'Shakespeare Key' two days
after, on the 18th March 1868, finishing
the latter on the 17th June 1872. These
nine years of steady, hard work were not
without their relief of pleasant recreations.
We had the pleasure of seeing many friends,
both those who resided in Italy and those
who were merely passing through Genoa
on their way to or from Rome, Florence,
etc. I kept a visitors' book wherein to
note these latter, its pages having three

columns; one for the name of the visitor, one for the name of the introducer, one for the date of the visit here. Besides seeing friends, we had much delightful music. My sister Sabilla got up some charming 'Mattinate,' for which she prepared the programme with the greatest care, selecting the most choice compositions of the best masters, and engaging the best available artists here for their due performance. With these were several of our friends, musically accomplished, and she always provided 'supplements' from her own family, in case of unforeseen disappointments from those whose names had been previously announced to sing or play. Thus, sometimes, my father's unaccompanied selections in the green books were given; at other times, Sabilla herself sang an aria, or Alfred a favourite bass song. Besides these home concerts (which took place in our picture gallery here), Sabilla wrote and got up some musical charades, sung and acted by ourselves and a few friends, which

were a decided success. A special musical
treat was enjoyed by us during that nine-
year interval, for in 1864 I had the delight
of hearing for the first time, and several
times after, Gounod's immortal opera of
'Faust,' given at the Carlo Felice Theatre
here. But at the close of that interval of
diligent, literary labour we gave ourselves
a complete holiday, going to Turin on the
17th July 1872, not returning home until
the 2d of September. While we were at
the then capital of Italy we took the opportunity of going through the then lately-
completed tunnel of the Mont Cenis Pass,
intending to make a short excursion into
France ; but when we arrived on the northern
side of the tunnel we found so utterly
break-down-looking a vehicle to convey us
from the station, that I hesitated to get
into it. Whereupon I heard the driver say
to his companion, '*Mais comment! cette
Dame ne veut pas monter dans cette belle
Calèche!*' We were offered the alternative
of mounting on mules, but to this caracoling

style of travel we preferred walking. The
inn at Modane, where we were to pass the
night before proceeding farther, proved to
be worthy of its '*belle Calèche*,' for we
ate through a positive haze of flies, and
slept in a room that was somewhat suggestive of a pigstye, as regards dirt and in-
convenience. We resolved to give up proceeding farther, and returned at once to
Turin, for we heard that there was a break
n the road between St Jean Maurienne
and St Michael. We enjoyed several delightful drives about the Turinese environs,
to Stupinigi, Veneria Reale, La Crocetta,
Rivoli, Moncalieri, and frequently by the
spacious Piazza 'Armi, beyond which was
a road that had, at one of its turnings, a
particularly graceful statue of a nymph at
a fountain. The museum, picture gallery
and the King's Garden were frequent haunts
of ours ; we were taken by one of its distinguished authorities, Signor Lumbroso, to
the Biblioteca del Re ; and we were so fortunate as to hear Mozart's charming opera,

'Cosi fan tutte,' very well performed at the Zerbino Theatre.

During the next few years we were not wholly idlers in the way of literary work. Charles wrote an article on 'The Old Schoolhouse at Enfield' for the 'St James's Magazine,' and we wrote together our ' Recollections of Writers,' which first appeared serially in successive numbers of the 'Gentleman's Magazine,' and subsequently was published in book form ; while I amused myself with writing verses, feeling encouraged to do so by the honour I had had some years before of Charles Dickens giving insertion in his 'All the Year Round' to two of my verse-stories, called 'The Yule Log' and 'Minnie's Musings,' besides six sonnets on 'Godsends,' and a few stanzas entitled 'Time's Healing.' In 1873 I wrote 'The Trust,' and 'The Remittance,' printed in England that year, and in America in 1874.

Having been requested to contribute to a charitable scheme in Rome, we wrote our

'Idyl of London Streets,' and sonnet on 'The Course of Time,' to be printed in Rome as a booklet for that purpose, and it appeared in 1875.

On the 15th of December 1876 my Charles's eighty-ninth birthday was celebrated by our family circle with even more than usual brightness—bright as his own ever-young nature. Verses from his wife, letters from friends at a distance, presence of friends living near, smiles from relatives around him, a huge cake lighted by wax tapers (eight green for the decades, nine white for the years), and, to crown all, favourite pieces from the green-bound music books sung to him by his nephews and nieces, made the day a supremely happy one. On the 19th of February 1877 we took our last walk together on the terrace, resting between whiles beneath the bay-laurel tree, and looking up gratefully at the clear, blue Italian sky.

On the 13th of March 1877, the

Charles Cowden Clarke.

spring   sun   shining   on   his   bed,   I
received   his   last   smile,   and   watched
beside   him   till   he   drew   his   last   breath.
The   marble   that   marked   his   grave   had
inscribed   on   one   of   its   sides   his   chosen
crest—an   oak-branch ;   his   chosen   motto—
'*Placidam   sub   libertate   quietem ;*'   his   name
and   the   date   of   his   birth   and   death ;   on
the   reverse   side   was   inscribed   his   own
characteristically   trustful,   cheerful-spirited

HIC JACET.

Let not a bell be toll'd, or tear be shed
              When I am dead ;
Let no night-dog, with dreary howl,
Or ghastly shriek of boding owl
Make harsh a change so calm, so hallowed ;
              Lay not my bed
'Mid yews and never-blooming cypresses,
              But under trees
Of simple flower and odorous breath,
The lime and dog-rose ; and beneath
Let primrose cups give up their honied lees
              To sucking bees,
Who all the shining day, while labouring,
              Shall drink and sing

A requiem o'er my peaceful grave.
For I would cheerful quiet have ;
Or, no noise ruder than the linnet's wing
          Or brook gurgling.
In harmony I've lived—so let me die,
That while 'mid gentler sounds this shell doth lie
The spirit aloft may float in spheral harmony.

That summer I was invited by Count Gigliucci and Clara to spend some weeks with them in their house at Fermo. I found it a truly interesting antique Italian mansion. On its ground floor was a suite of apartments, adjoining each other in the style of royal palaces—a billiard-room, an ante-room, a ball-room, a music-room, etc., etc. A staircase built in the thickness of a wall led up to an upper range of rooms, where the family lived their daily domestic life. A private chapel formed part of the edifice ; and once, when Clara took me down to the basement portion of the house, I saw a highly-ornate sedan chair, which used to convey ancestral countesses Gigliucci to the church or to the opera—for there was a spacious opera-house and a stately cathedral. The cathedral is on the summit of the hill on which Fermo is situate, and it is a very fine and large cathedral for so small a town as Fermo. Along the upper range of rooms above alluded to, there runs a long and wide corridor, at one end of which is a colossal window, commanding a noble view of the Appenines, including the mountain known as the ' *Gran sasso d'Italia.*' The front of the house faces towards the champaigne, stretching down the hill's descent until it reaches the Adriatic Sea, dotted by fishing vessels with their variously-coloured sails.

Anything more hospitably affectionate and solicitously careful to soothe my thoughts than the reception I met with from my dear ones in this picturesque spot cannot be imagined. My sister Clara, when I had rested a day after my journey, asked me if I would like her to sing to me. With joy I accepted, and we adjourned at once downstairs to the music - room, called 'the red drawing-room.' Clara bade

me choose the song I should best like to
hear her sing first, and I chose her Westminster Abbey festival song 'How beautiful are the feet,' its angelic promise bringing
balm to the soul. She generously went on
to the recitatives in the Messiah, and then
sang Mozart's lovely 'Deh vieni e non
tardar,' her voice just its own unrivalled
beauty of tone, pure in style, potent in
appeal to the heart.

After that first evening of musical bliss
I had many more, for Clara sang to me,
accompanied by her daughter Porzia, who,
with her sister Valeria, gave me many
delicious treats of favourite vocal and
pianoforte duets. I never heard Clara
say, 'Shall we go down into the red
drawing-room?' but a thrill of joy ran
through me, and were I to enumerate
all the enchanting things she sang for me,
or that her two daughters sang and
played for me, the reader would envy me
the time I spent so delightfully at Fermo.
One afternoon's music I must recur to,

for the sake of the picture it gave me. One of the Gigliucci cousins, Conte Geppino Vinci, brought his violin, and accompanied Clara in Spohr's song 'When this scene of trouble closes,' and Guglielmi's 'Gratias agimus,' Porzia playing the piano-forte accompaniment. The little baby Vinci having been brought and laid upon a cushion at her father's feet, she looked up at him, listening to the music and cooing soft approval ; the entire group thus affording a regale for eye as well as ear. Another very southern picture was enjoyed by me there. One forenoon Clara called to me to come into the cor-ridor, that I might see one of their peasant girls, who had brought her (according to the Italian custom among a proprietor's tenantry, and which Shakespeare has so appropriately introduced in his 'Merchant of Venice,' where old Gobbo brings 'a dish of doves' as an intended present to his son's master, Shylock) a basket of fruit. There stood the girl, her black

eyes and hair beneath a bright kerchief,
her gleaming white teeth, snowy bodice,
her coloured apron and striped skirt, and
the rich tint of the apricots in her basket,
formed a glowing portrait not to be forgotten by me.   Several delightful drives
were taken for me and with me, by the
Count and Clara, through fields and vine-
yards belonging to his tenantry ; and once
I was taken to a magnificent old oak
tree, beneath which I was allowed to stand
and gather a spray of oak, similar to a
' chosen crest ' I knew and loved.   On my
return home to Genoa, when I chanced
to be speaking to my sister Sabilla of my
liking for Northern air, and of my weak-
ened eyes, she proposed that we should
take a journey together to Coblentz, where
lived a celebrated oculist, whom I could
consult.   I answered, ' Why not ? ' and
thus summarily was this journey agreed
upon, so summarily, too, was it put into
practice, that we set forth a day or two
after taking the route by the Mont Cenis

Pass, to Basle, where, as we sat at tea
and supper, I told Sabilla that I already
felt the beneficial influence of the Northern
air, its freshness, its invigorating quality,
for I ate with better appetite than I had
done for months past. On arriving at
Coblentz we took up our abode at pleasant
Pension Ernen. It was close to our
oculist's house ; it was on the road from
the town, its garden abutted on the delightful *Anlagen* by the side of the river
Rhine, an *Anlagen* specially patronised by
the Empress Augusta, who contributed
funds to its proper and tasteful keeping
up, and who visited it often. It was
shaded by trees, it had a *Restauration*,
where people drank coffee and ate cakes,
and was here and there adorned by
sculptured figures and groups of vases.
We frequently walked there, and many
times made it our way to entering the
town. Once, while sitting quietly on one
of the numerous seats placed in recesses
there, we had the pleasure of seeing a

woodpecker make its way up the bole of a tree, and actually 'tapping' the bark as he proceeded clingingly towards its branches.

Our hostess, Fräulein Ernen, was admirably fitted for her vocation, careful of the comfort and well-being of her boarders —almost all of them patients of our oculist. At the very Teutonic early dinner-hour of two o'clock, we found at the table several pleasant, chatty people, among whom was Mr Henley, the artist, his seat being next mine. He courteously addressed me, and told me many entertaining anecdotes of the persons who had been his sitters for their portraits—royal personages and others. Among them he mentioned Nathaniel Hawthorne, saying he was so sensitive a sitter that the most timid young girl did not surpass him in shyness. On our visit to the famous oculist he pronounced that my eyes required daily dropping into them a certain remedy, therefore daily we visited him. We found

him a lively, almost boyish-mannered man,
but kindly and skilful. As a specimen
of the former characteristic, once, on my
happening to say that I had never heard
the famous song 'Die Wacht am Rhein,'
that created such universal enthusiasm at the
time of the German war, he (having been
in one of its campaigns) immediately sang
the song for me at full voice, and flourish-
ing the camel-hair pencil he was using
for applying the remedy to my eyes, with
outstretched arm on high. As a specimen
of his kindliness of nature, when I chanced
to speak of the lovely, tender scene of
young Prince Arthur pleading for his
eyes to be spared from burning by
Hubert, in Shakespeare's play of 'King
John,' our oculist took down a German
version of the tragedy and read the scene
aloud with tears in his eyes. At another
time he laughingly recounted to us how
he had bought a blind horse, cured it
himself, and found it a useful steed during
the campaign and ever after.

During our stay at Coblentz, we renewed our acquaintance with Madame Rosa Mendelssohn, whom we had known at Nice, while she and her husband had been staying there for a short time. She and her niece, Miss Thormann, received us most cordially, and the visit was a memorable one. In the room where we first went there was an interesting bas-relief medallion - portrait (size of life) of the then lately deceased Professor Benjamin Mendelssohn, her husband. Each side of the medallion were pots of ivy, trained up to surround the head like a wreath or garland. The dining-room was delightful, bowed in shape, the front with windows looking towards the pretty road in which the house stood, the back with a wide door opening on a staircase that led divergingly to the garden at the rear of the house, and this door was kept wide open all the time we dined, so that it seemed as though we were dining in an arbour. In the room was a cuckoo-

clock that chimed its fluting notes while
we ate our dainty dinner, which included
Rhine salmon and roast venison. After
dinner we took coffee in the music-room,
and as we passed into it, we crossed
through a smaller one, where hung an
interesting water-colour sketch by Felix
himself — a view of that very village of
Horchheim (where we then were visiting),
as seen from its music-room window.
Miss Thormann—an accomplished amateur
pianist—played several of Felix's 'Lieder,'
one or two of Schumann's, compositions,
and a little - known Beethoven Sonata.
Mention having been made by Madame
Mendelssohn and Miss Thormann of a
concert to be given at Ems by 'a wonderful young Spanish violinist' — Pablo di
Sarasate — Sabilla invited both ladies to
go over with her to Ems and hear the
concert, but as Madame Mendelssohn de-
clined making the exertion, Miss Thormann only accepted.

Of course we took many a delightful

walk and drive to the various enchanting spots on the banks of the Rhine
within easily accessible distances, among
others to a village on the opposite side
of the river (the road to which passed
near to the fortress of Ehrenbreitstein)
called Ahrenberg, where we found a
pretty little church, its interior fitted up
with tasteful candelabra in the form of
lilies and leaves in their natural colours,
and some grotto - work.   Another excursion was a drive to Gülz on the river
Mosel, where we crossed the ferry in
our carriage, and returned by the opposite
side to Coblentz.   When we went to
take leave of Madame Rosa Mendelssohn,
we saw Felix's younger daughter and her
five children.   One of them, a little baby,
had its fingers placed by Sabilla on the
pianoforte as if playing, as she said that
Felix's grandchild ought early to accustom
its hands to that position.   We left
Coblentz on the 30th September, took
similar route back, and arrived in Genoa

on the 4th October. We had much home-
music, and I heard Patti when she sang
in the 'Barbiere di Siviglia' here in
that year; and on March 11th, 1878,
Sabilla and I went for a change to Rome.
Of the grandeurs there I saw but few in
comparison with those we were com-
pelled to leave unseen, for a gentleman
who was asked in what time Rome could
be thoroughly visited, said,— 'I can't
say, for I have lived in Rome only forty
years.' But we enjoyed many of its
noblest picture galleries. We, of course,
did not fail to make a pilgrimage to
dear John Keats's tomb, neighboured by
that of glorious Shelley's heart, and we
took more than one drive out into the
picturesque Campagna.

One of our very first visits was paid to
the American minister, George Perkins
Marsh, who had been so generous as to
have lent us his rare copy of Florio's 'Second
Frutes' while we were editing our 'Annotated Shakespeare.' This curious work of

Florio's, on our careful examination of it,
caused us to feel sure that it (as well as
Florio's Italian and English Dictionary) had
been well known to, and much used by,
Shakespeare himself. Mr Marsh was a
distinguished philologist, besides being an
able statesman. He had been thoroughly
appreciated and frequently conversed with
by the amiable and highly-accomplished
Queen Margaret, who is one of the most
gracious of sovereigns. At Mrs Marsh's
receptions we were more than once gratified
visitors, and met there several distinguished
persons. She had long been an affectionate
friend of Clara and her two daughters, asking the two latter to make tea and preside
at her afternoon tea-table on many occasions
of these receptions. We also made the
acquaintance of Miss Brewster, a descendant
of the Brewster who had been one of the
patriots that sailed in the 'Mayflower,' when
the ship left England and arrived at the
Plymouth Rock in America. She showed
us a tea-set that had been fac-similed from

the one used aboard that renowned vessel.
While we were in Rome we enjoyed some
special music. A concert given by Signor
Sgambati, the most exquisite of Italian
pianists. Another concert given for a
charitable purpose, wherein a lady (born a
Russian princess, but married to a German
professor) played on the pianoforte in
masterly style, and on which occasion,
Madame Ristori recited (I may say, acted)
the sleeping-scene of Lady Macbeth, sup-
ported by a lady and gentleman who represented the waiting-gentlewoman and the
doctor. To show how careful really great
artists are, I may mention that Ristori asked
my sister Clara to hear her recite and
rehearse this scene before she performed it
at the concert.

An early and memorable visit Sabilla and
I paid to Joseph Severn, the generous-hearted
artist who gave up his then engagements
to accompany his friend, John Keats, to
Italy, when the young poet was in a decline
that ended in his death. We found Severn

himself on a sick - bed, arranged in his studio, and opposite to him, the portrait he was painting from memory, when taken ill, of Keats, still so dear to him. He spoke to us cheerily, and with interest, of all that most engaged the thoughts of us three.

On our return home to Genoa from Rome, we resumed our usual life of home music and home occupations ; but in June, having received an invitation from our kind friends, Mr and Mrs Littleton, to visit them, we left for England. During my stay there I superintended the bringing out of our ' Recollections of Writers,' then in course of printing in book-form. We visited our favourite English picture collections—the choice one at the Dulwich Gallery ; the ever-beautiful National Gallery, where we found some fine additions, such as the Turner collection, etc. ; and at the Aquarium we saw gathered together some of George Cruik-shank's admirable illustrations ; though I own I regretted not seeing among them those

he made for my 'Kit Bam's Adventures.'
We paid a visit to Lady Shelley, who was
then at her town-house on the Chelsea Em-
bankment. She invited us to go and see
her at Boscombe, where she and Sir Percy
had collected most interesting relics of his
illustrious father; but, unfortunately, we
were unable to accept the invitation. On
our way back from England we visited the
Paris Exhibition of that year, and spent a
fortnight at Aix-les-Bains, where we heard
a fine instrumental concert given by the
orchestra from the Regio Teatro at Turin,
and were taken by a friend into the Gambling Room, in which we saw two fanatic
players seated at the gambling - table, to
secure places, an hour beforehand, and
on our returning after the concert we
saw these wretched gentlemen, with excited eyes and burning red cheeks, deep
in play.

In July 1879, Sabilla and I resolved to
go and enjoy the Mozart Musical Festival
at Salzburg, inviting our niece Porzia to

accompany us, and a great enjoyment it
proved.   Our visit thither being exactly
fifty years after my father's, to take the subscribed sum to Madame Sonnenberg, the
great composer's sister, we were received
with marked kindliness by the authorities
there, and shown particular attention.

As a fitting commencement to the festival,
I went a pilgrimage to the house where
Mozart was born, the font whereat he was
baptised, and the dwelling where he lived,
loved and wrote.   A gay look of jubilee and
bright expectancy pervaded the streets, where
long pennons and flags of all colours hung
floating from upper windows and reached to
ground floors ; while troops of visitors from
all parts flocked through the thoroughfares
in holiday travelling trim.   On the evening
of 17th July, when the first of the three days'
concerts took place, a large company was
assembled in the 'Aula Academica,' where
the executants were already stationed in their
places cn the platform, and 'ready-tuned.'
The very first chord of Mozart's finest over-

ture served well to announce the supremacy
of the famed Vienna Orchestra. Herr Hans
Richter presided as conductor ; and a more
excellent one it has never been my good
fortune to hear—though I have heard Michael
Costa, Chelard and Felix Mendelssohn themselves. Beethoven's Seventh Symphony, with
its sublimely poetical slow movement and exquisitely playful Scherzo, closed the evening's
musical feast. The day's enjoyment harmon-
ised well with the evening's entertainment ;
for a town of choicer loveliness in situation
and scenery is rarely to be seen. Placed on
the banks of a rapid stream, the River Sal-
bach, surrounded by green heights and distant mountains, well-wooded slopes on which
picturesque castles and lordly mansions are
perched, shores along which brightly and
variously-coloured houses range in the neat-
ness and grace of adornment that characterises
German dwellings—this spot forms an endless
succession of pictures and charming land-
scapes, besides affording scope for enchanting
drives amid lanes and woodlands. As a final

M

touch—which would have rejoiced the heart
of Walter Scott himself, who knew, none
better, that good fare crowns befittingly the
enjoyment of Nature's romantic scenery and
refined art pleasure—the eating in Salzburg
was of the best ; trout that would have
had Isaac Walton's cordial commendation,
chickens delicate and 'tender as morning
dew,' with Alpine butter and fresh cream,
made each day's repast a feast worthy of
the 'Musikfest' at night. On the morning
of 18th July there was an open-air entertainment on the Kapuzinerberg, consisting of a
four-part song for men's voices, an address
delivered by Herr Baumeister, a celebrated
actor who had a grand speaking voice, with
fervour of delivery and excellent enunciation. The touching words he poured forth,
in powerful tones, were so sonorous that
they reached the opposite hills, which echoed
back the praises of our divine Mozart with
thrilling effect.

On reaching the point of the Capucin
Hill, where a small summer-house stands,

I found an eager crowd assembled, some in the full blaze of the sunshine, under parasols and umbrellas, some seeking scraps of shade skirting the enclosure, some clustering beneath the adjoining trees, and a fortunate few on a rickety wooden bench under the eaves of a wood-cutter's cottage Committee gentlemen came to my sister Sabilla and myself, asking us to enter the summer-house, which had the peculiar interest of being the actual spot where Mozart composed his opera of 'Die Zauberflöte.' It is fitted up with exact models of the table at which he wrote, and of the chair in which he sat when occupying this summer-house. Its walls are hung round with pictures, photographs and innumerable tributary wreaths ; on the table lay an open Mozart album, in which we were requested to inscribe our names, as the daughters of Vincent Novello, who, exactly half a century before, this very month, in the July of 1829, came to

Salzburg to convey to Mozart's sister (then in failing health and means) a sum of money subscribed by the musical professors of London as a testimony of their admiration for the great composer's genius, and of their sympathy with his sister in her declining age. Strangely moving was it to stand beneath the little summerhouse roof, looking forth upon the very mountains and woods and river and picturesque town that Mozart beheld when he raised his eyes from his MS. ; strange to sit in the chair he occupied, listening to the strains he composed ; strange to be in the very place where, fifty years before, my own father had come to visit the birthplace of his favourite composer, and the spot which had witnessed the birth of some of that composer's finest compositions. With reverential humility we complied with the committee's request, and placed in the Mozart album our photographs and the following inscriptions :—

'I pray you let us satisfy our eyes (and ears)
    With the memorials and things of fame
    That do renown this city.'
SHAKESPEARE's ' Twelfth Night,' Act. III. Scene 3.
  *Mary   Victoria   Cowden - Clarke   (born
  Novello).*—Salzburg, July 1879.

IMPROMPTU ACROSTIC.

S alzburg, for ever will thy name recall
A pleasant mem'ry to my mind ; when all
B ut as a dream of beauty shall appear
I llumined by art's glow, remote but clear ;
L ov'd Mozart seems to tread thy busy streets,
L ost though he be to mortal ken, he meets
A t ev'ry moment my admiring eyes.

N ot like the empty visions that arise
O ut of the misty past.   No, Mozart lives
V ividly present, while his music gives
E ternal rapture, ever freshly born,
L ovely as Spring, as radiant as the morn.
L ong as art love shall exist, Mozart's name
O 'er all shall triumph in the rolls of fame.
                Salzburg, July 18th, 1879.

Schumann's two glorious compositions, the
' Andante and Variationen,' and Quintette completed the intense satisfaction afforded to us

by this truly delightful 'Salzburger Musikfest.'

From Salzburg we went to Vienna, where
our first delight was hearing an evening
service in the glorious cathedral. The lovely
Gothic interior, the blaze of silver (with gold
rays from the centre) of the rich altar-piece,
the kneeling priests in white and gold vest-
ments, the warm colouring of the stained-
glass windows, with the general low light of
the arched stone walls just revealing the many
antique monuments that abound there, all
thoroughly enchanted me. An early visit
we of course paid to the Belvedere Gallery,
containing whole rooms full of Rubens, that
make one wonder how a man's life could
suffice to cover so much canvas with so much
magnificent painting, and with such noble
poetry of his imagination, besides being an
ambassador. A room full of Velasquez, with
portraits of children deliciously true to *aristo-
cratic nature*, a picture of Murillo's—a boy St
John with a lamb—exquisite. A lovely little
low long picture by Domenico Feti (a painter

I had never heard of before). The death of
Leander, and the despair of Hero, charmingly
poetical in idea and treatment ; in short,
room after room of beauties and riches innumerable. Another small gallery, consisting but of three rooms, at the Schonborn
Palace, kept us lingering by a Canaletto quite
astounding for truth to nature, and open-air
effect, with perfect perspective—of a house
and grass plot towards the right-hand front
of the picture, and another house rather back-
wards. In the Lichtenstein Gallery, besides
the numerous treasures of Vandyke, Rembrandt and Rubens that it contains, we came
upon a bewitching picture by the last-named
artist, a Perseus and Andromeda, with little
Loves flying about, two trying to mount
Pegasus, two helping to unfasten the chains
of Andromeda, etc., etc., all of them exquisite.

When we left Vienna we went up to
Dresden, which I at once named, and ever
after spoke of, as ' Delightful Dresden.' The
store of riches, crown jewels, precious crystals,
etc., in the ' Green Vault ' there, was not half

so attractive to us as the picture gallery, where we were almost daily haunters of its rooms.

Many a drive we took in the charming 'Grosse Garten' and into the country beyond, visiting several of the picturesque environs that abound in the vicinity. We frequently made our way to the public square in front of the palace to hear a fine military band playing in one of its angles ; and on the first occasion of our doing this, were so struck with the beauty of the performance, its admirably breathed out pianos, its perfect crescendos, and precision of *togetherhood*, that I could not resist the temptation to applaud ; and, catching the bandmaster's eye, I clapped my hands obviously. He, with brisk military promptitude, raised his hand to his helmet, saluted and smiled, with a little sudden bow, as our carriage passed on rapidly. One evening, soon after our arrival, we went to the Sommertheater in the Grosse Garten, where was performed a piece entitled 'Die Kinder des Capitan Grant,' which entertained me be-

yond words, as a perfect reminder of my old
Coburg and Surrey theatre times. A captain
and his boy son left to perish on a desert
island by a treacherous mate and crew, a bottle
(containing news of their condition) miracul-
ously reaching their friends in a castle in
Glasgow. The said friends, with their comic
servant and the two other children of Captain
Grant (a boy and a girl) setting off in a yacht
to save their esteemed Captain Grant ; their
various adventures on reaching South America ;
Mexican guides, false and faithless, leading
them where a volcano bursts, and its lava in-
terrupts their path ; a mysterious Patagonian
chief (who expresses himself in fluent *Hoch
Deutsch*), friendly and protective, and who dies
from having heroically sucked the poison from
a snake-bite in the girl child's leg ; attacks of
wild Indians, shouts, pistol-shots innumerable
(in fact, from what I could make out, pistol-
shots were invariably introduced when extra
excitement and interest and *row* were needed) ;
more wanderings ; a dance of ballet-girls and
men with lanterns in a Mexican temple fes-

tivity; a sudden remorse and reform of the 'treacherous mate,' who turns up at the most unexpected moment, and offers to conduct the search party to the exact spot where he abandoned Captain Grant and his son; a change of scene to a desolate part of the desert island, with Captain Grant and his son at the last extremity of starvation and cold, an iceberg having closed them in from the open sea and their last hope of rescue; an affecting scene (really prettily done) of the father half resolving to shorten the sufferings of his exhausted and sleeping son by stabbing him with the knife he still has; his last appeal to Heaven with the boy kneeling beside him—when the mid-scene of iceberg draws away, and the yacht is seen approaching in full sail. 'God save the Queen' is played, the party of friends rush on, and the curtain falls amid general meeting and happiness.

The very next day a quite different series of theatrical entertainments commenced for us. The opening of the Hoftheater for that season was announced to take place in the evening,

the performance being 'Die Wiederspenstige.'
I heard this title with indifference, but what
was my awakened interest when, asking
Sabilla to explain, she told me this piece was
the German version of Shakespeare's 'Taming
of the Shrew.' We then of course immediately took stalls, and went to what proved
the beginning of an Elysium of play-
going; not only then, but in several subsequent visits to 'Delightful Dresden.' The
Hoftheater itself is lofty, spacious, cool,
airy; the performances commence punctually
at seven, allowing return home seldom later
than ten o'clock. The scenery superb; the
artists—dramatic and vocal—excellent; the
pieces chosen are artistically instructive,
as well as artistically interesting, being al-
ternately dramatic and operatic; the former
selected from the best dramatists, the latter
selected from composers of classic celebrity,
besides those of more modern date; so that
the audience becomes more cultivated in
dramatic authorship and in musical composition of various styles. On that first

evening we beheld two admirable performers, Dettmer as Petruchio, Ellmenreich as Katharina. His acting was entirely to my taste; giving the assumed harshness of dictatorship with (in soliloquy) the real liking that Petruchio has for his chosen wife. His speaking voice equalled that of Salvini for beauty and richness of tone. Ellmenreich was charming, and proved to be equally so in characters she subsequently played—of high tragic, or genteel comedy impersonation. We became such inveterate playgoers that, during the more than two months of our stay in Dresden, we scarcely missed a single evening of performance. But besides our theatre music, we enjoyed many a magnificent mass of Mozart and other composers at the Hofkirche; and several admirably sung motetts, etc., by well-trained boy singers at the Lutheran Vesper Service in the Kreuzkirche. The precision and perfectly in tune singing of those boys in unaccompanied pieces by Bach, Mendelssohn and other composers, was a delight to hear.

One evening we went to hear a concert of Hungarians (announced in the programme as 'Zigeuner-Kapelle Farkas More aus Budapest'), which was an extraordinarily interesting thing to hear. National, peculiar, very wild, three of the pieces were called 'Czardas,' and were especially curious. Rapid and eccentric in the extreme; and in two of them a young violinist of the party executed what seemed to be an impetuous improvised recitative movement, accompanied by merely two violins, a viola (extraordinarily large in size) and violoncello; while at its close, the whole orchestra (including double bass, clarinet, oboe, and a very large zithern, admirably played), joined in like a choral conclusion.

On leaving Dresden we made Eger our first halting-place, in order to make a pilgrimage to the house where Wallenstein was murdered; because we had seen Schiller's 'Wallenstein' magnificently got up at the Dresden Hoftheater. We found the spot (the Rathhaus) where the murder took place grim and quaint enough to be quite in keeping with its tradition ; an old half-Gothic portal giving entrance to a dingy old courtyard, round which were stuck various carved stones and rude images of old German warriors and monumental records of their doings ; a balustraded gallery of dark wood running round the courtyard interior of the first floor— like our old English inn yards. On the left side, beneath the huge portal, was an entrance door standing open, where at once ascends the antique staircase so well represented in the scene of ' Wallenstein's Tod ' at the Hoftheater. The artistic scene-painter there must have gone himself to Eger and taken a sketch of the actual spot, and then enlarged it for stage representation—the effect was so true, and yet so picturesquely improved.

We made a short stay at Munich that we might renew the acquaintance Sabilla and I had made with the Art Galleries of the

Pinacotek and Glyptothek on our return journey from England in 1862. The International Exhibition at Munich was open at the time of our second visit, but although it consisted entirely of paintings and sculpture, I did not find a single specimen that I should have cared to possess. Sabilla and Porzia were able to procure tickets for a performance at the Opera House of Wagner's 'Gotterdämmerung;' but I preferred staying quietly indoors, looking out upon the open square, beyond which I could see the towers of the quaint old Frauenkirche, lighted by the setting sun and gradually by the crescent moon and single planet star, while I thought of the many blessings I had in my long life to compensate for its sorrows.

We returned to Genoa by the Brenner Pass; where, instead of the snow and ice which we were told we should encounter, we found sunshine, blue sky and charming transit through lovely green Tyrol.

In 1880 our villa was honoured by a

visit from the Kronprinzessin of Germany, then staying at Pegli. Her Royal Highness was graciously interested by a portrait of our sister Clara, painted by Magnus of Berlin, who had given lessons in painting to Her Royal Highness,—herself a proficient in that art.

Having been so gratified by our German tour of 1879, we resolved to go thither the very next year ; so, after paying a delightful visit to friends at Stresa, on the Lago Maggiore, we went up to Nuremberg, where we saw Albert Dürer's studio, preserved just in the state it was when he worked there ; and an exhibition of Kranach's antique paintings, where the custodian was an old woman with a head precisely like one of Kranach's epoch, so queer and antiquated was it.

At Bamberg we visited an admirable lady pianist, a friend of ours years before in England, who played to us again with quite her former excellence. She was peculiarly great in Beethoven's Sonatas, all

of which she knew by heart. We made
some stay at Cassel; making our first
visit to the picture gallery there, which is
rich in Rembrandts. Our drives were frequent and delightful. One, from Wilhelms-
thal to Wilhelmshöhe through magnificent
woods, remains vividly in my memory;
for, on approaching the former-named
palace as we drove up the avenue leading thereto, we saw a large party of
gentlemen picnicing under the trees; who,
when they saw us approaching, made animated. signs to the coachman to halt. Then
one of the gentlemen flew to the side of
the carriage, bearing in his hand a superb-
sized foaming tankard, which he presented
to us ladies, and from which each of us
ladies in turn drank from, I exclaiming,
'*Lebe hoch, Deutschland!*' The gentleman
smiled and looked delighted (indeed, he
and his whole party seemed in exuberant
spirits, but went through the ceremony in
the highest good taste and politeness), and
then he handed the tankard up to the

N

coachman, who quaffed it off with abundant relish. As we drove away the band which was with the party sounded a flourish of trumpets in honour of us. Altogether we thought it a pretty characteristic and most *German* incident.

One morning early, while we were at Cassel, what should greet our delighted ears before we were up, but a charming serenade given by the military band to their general, who lived next door to us. First a magnificent chorale—simple in its strain, but full of the most enchanting chords, breathed out entrancingly, with the most exquisite precision of tune, the most perfect togetherhood in beginning and ending phrases ; the most true and intense feeling for due expression in sentiment ; next was played a brisk Hungarian dance, then a quick march ; and lastly a very brilliant piece, the subject with which it commenced being taken from the padlock song in Mozart's 'Zauberflöte.' From Cassel we went up to Berlin. My experience of

the Prussian capital was not very favour-
able ; for constant rain prevailed during
most of our time there, preventing our
enjoying as much as we could have
desired to visit. But the picture gallery,
the museum, and Rauch's Studio afforded
us much art pleasure ; while a drive to
the park and mausoleum of Charlotten-
burg was extremely interesting to us. And
we were so fortunate as to see Otto
Devrient play Mephistopheles, in his own
adaptation for the stage of Goethe's 'Second
Part of Faust.' His acting was perfection,
and marvellous in appropriate diabolism.
One touch particularly struck us. In the
scene where there is a royal reception,
Devrient's face suddenly changed to a look
of shuddering disgust ; and we then perceived that it was when a train of ecclesi-
astics and robed bishops entered the presence.
Otto Devrient was one of that famous family
of Devrients who for years had been first-
rate actors and actresses. I had seen
Madame Schroeder-Devrient during the

first performance of the German company in London ; had seen Emile Devrient play Faust at the St James's Theatre there ; and I had seen a younger Devrient play Sebastian in Shakespeare's 'Twelfth Night' in Dresden. Yearnings of remembrance of this last-named city seized us, and we left Berlin for 'Delightful Dresden.' On arrival we found finer weather to add to our exhilaration at finding ourselves again in our favourite Saxon capital. The season at the Hoftheater had just commenced, and we at once plunged into the old enjoyment of theatre-going every evening ; punctual attendance at the Hofkirche for High Mass, and at the Kreuzkirche vesper service, where the boy choir was so excellent, etc., etc. A few changes had taken place there since our previous visit. Ellmenreich was married, but still remained on the stage. A delicious baritone, Degele, was singing in various parts with excellent effect ; while the acting of Dettmer as Macduff in Shakespeare's 'Macbeth,' de-

serves special record. I can never forget
him in the grand scene of the fourth act,
where news is brought to him of his wife
and children being put to death by the
tyrant. It was the truest and most affecting expression of manly anguish I ever
beheld. His fine flexible voice, with its
power of breaking when expressing strong
emotion, aided him to perfection, and his
gestures were profoundly indicative of
mental torture, without a tinge of exaggeration. Dettmer had the curious gift
of being able to *turn pale* (a gift I have
heard was possessed by the French actor
Talma), and at the passage where Malcolm
says :—' Ne'er pull your hat upon your
brows ; give sorrow words,'—when the hat
was removed Dettmer's face was deathly
white.

To give an idea of Ellmenreich's varied
power in acting, I may mention that her
Viola in Shakespeare's ' Twelfth Night ' was
bewitchingly playful ; while her impersonation of Goethe's Gretchen in the first part

of 'Faust' was profoundly moving. Pure,
innocent, winningly childlike, happy at first ;
broken, despairing, lost at last. Her madness,
while Faust weeps with remorse at her feet,
was perfectly haunting, and really affected
Sabilla and me for a long time after.

A very interesting day was spent by us,
when we went to visit the 'Saxon Switzerland.' We were favoured by fine weather ;
we drove by the left banks of the River
Elbe, crossed the ferry at Pilnitz, proceeded
by a gentle rise all the way through picturesque villages and amid fine views. We
passed the day on the fine cliff called the
'Bastei,' wandering about among its rocky
summits, conveniently made accessible by
connecting bridges and well-kept paths. Another excursion was to Meissen, where we
ascended the crag on which are perched the
antique cathedral and castle.

A particularly interesting ceremony we
witnessed (from a window), which took
place on the Altmarkt Platz of Dresden.
The edges of the large platz were literally

crammed with people, windows and roofs,
even, were full of excited gazers, while the
central space was marked off by gigantic
festoons of green wreaths surmounted by
close, bead-like rows of white lamps (green
and white being the colours of Saxony), beneath which rose a wooden amphitheatre of
seats erected for the reception of the
relations of those who had fallen at Sedan
(the day being the anniversary of the
victory obtained there). Within this amphitheatre was an open space, where gradually
assembled various processions, civic and
military, with their several bands of music
and some hundreds of young ladies wearing white, and sashes of the national colours
with garlands of oak leaves on their heads.
The sight of these falling in, two by two,
and forming a long line round the statue
in the centre, and extending towards the
throned and crimson-laid stand prepared for
the King and Queen of Saxony and their
Court, was extremely beautiful; the more
so, as most of these fair girlish heads had

magnificent tresses of hair falling from their green wreaths on to their shoulders and down their backs.

Precisely as the clock struck eleven, the royal carriages drove up, and as the Court party alighted and took their places beneath the canopy, the whole assembly cheered, waved hats and handkerchiesfs, while the bands struck up 'God save the Queen' (the German national air being the same as ours). Then the chorus of young ladies and of students (also wearing chaplets on their heads) sang Handel's grand 'Hallelujah Chorus' with fine effect ; a speech was delivered to the King by a Dresden magnate ; Wagner's stately and effective 'Kaiser Marsch' was played by the united bands ; and, at a signal, the tall draperies around the central statue were rapidly lowered, and the 'Germania' was displayed to view amid universal cheering and waving of hats and handkerchiefs. Lastly, the King and Queen and Court party stepped down from their daïs, and walked round the central space amid more cheering and waving, and closely examined the statue and the green wreaths which the young ladies had placed upon the steps at its base. After this, the royalties stepped into their carriage-and-four, driving off amid acclamations.

We had made acquaintance with three amiable American ladies—a mother and two daughters; the mother almost as fresh-complexioned and young looking as her daughters. One of the daughters was taking lessons in pianoforte playing, the other in singing. These two young ladies flew into our room one afternoon with a couple of white rosebuds in their hand, which they presented to Sabilla and me in token of the pleasure they had just had in reading my two verse stories, 'The Trust' and 'The Remittance.' The young lady who was then studying singing was no other than Miss Agnes Huntington, who subsequently made so successful an operatic career in London and in America.

We witnessed in the Grosse Garten an

interesting celebration of the 'Albertverein Fest.' In the large space near the lake, a kind of tent-temple had been erected for the royalties; and immediately on the verge of the sheet of water, seats had been arranged for the Court party. In the middle of the lake a large flat stage, placed across and upon several firmly-moored barges, was visible to the thousands who stood on the banks, forming a variegated edge on the green sward around the water. On the moored stage, acrobats, slack-rope dancers, etc., etc., displayed their feats, and could be seen by the Court and the crowd most conveniently. There were military bands stationed at regular distances in the gardens; and there were stalls held by celebrities and by ladies and gentlemen, where toys and knick-knacks were sold for the charity. One of these stalls was held by a clever comic actor named Löber, who caused shouts of laughter as he humorously disposed of stacks and stacks of gingerbread to eager purchasers.

So perfect was the order maintained, yet the freedom allowed, that Sabilla and I were able to walk leisurely behind the platform on which the royalties were seated; and when they descended the steps thereof, and got into their carriages, we were standing within fifty paces from them. No pushing, no elbowing among the crowd; but quiet and orderly they stood, just raising their hats respectfully as the King and Queen passed. In the evening there was a performance in the Sommertheater, at which the royalties were present. The King and Queen laughed heartily, and came in quite simple fashion to that small barn of a theatre, seeming thoroughly to enjoy themselves. We were close to them, and could see the Queen's sweet and amiable face completely well. We were told that she took special interest in the particular charity for which this 'Gartenfest' was got up each year; so that she made a point of enjoying its gaieties with her people.

We took our leave of 'Delightful Dresden'

and its unrivalled Hoftheater with a piece called 'Prinz Friedrich von Homburg,' in which my admirable Dettmer played to perfection, and Ellmenreich was her usual graceful and fascinating self. In one of its scenes, Dettmer had occasion to introduce most appropriately his singular power of *turning pale* in a moment of intense emotion, so that I was more than ever convinced of his possessing this gift, and also more than ever charmed with his full and touching voice.

The next year, 1881, was marked by quite different, though quite as interesting, experiences. Sabilla and I were invited by our friends, Mr and Mrs Littleton, to visit them again ; but as their house in Sydenham was undergoing complete restoration, they were staying in London for the first portion of our return to England. This afforded an opportunity for us to hear some charming recitals of Rubinstein, who was giving a series in the St James's Hall. This was an especial treat for me.

I, who had heard all the most celebrated
pianists for years at the Philharmonic Society
(of which my father was one of the original
instigators and first members, and had taken
me regularly to hear its concerts, ever since
I was quite a young girl), John Cramer,
Thalberg, Döhler, Pauer, etc., etc., felt
extreme eagerness to hear Rubenstein, of
whom I had often heard, but whom I had
never heard play. What especially charmed
me in his playing that season was the extremely appropriate and characteristic style
in which he played the respective compositions of each composer he selected for performance at his several recitals. I felt, so
to say, as if he played Mozart, Mozartianly ;
Beethoven, Beethovenishly ; Weber, Weber-
ishly, and so on, while his own compositions he delivered with a spirit and effect
that appeared to me to be peculiarly suited
to them. I particularly admired his own
manner ; no breaking the time, no exag-
gerated tricks.

One day Mr Littleton went with me to

the South Kensington Museum, and helped me to find the façade of the dear old school-house at Enfield, which had been placed in what were called 'The Exhibition Buildings,' and was beautifully preserved ; the pome-granate garlands and the cherub heads being quite complete.

On my birthday a delightful surprise had been prepared for me. My kind friend Mr Littleton had had printed for me my verse volume of 'Honey from the Weed,' and he brought me the first bound copy as a birthday pleasure. Its graceful and ap-propriate cover—ferns and weeds, with a bee hovering over them extracting their sweets — had been designed by his son, Mr Alfred Littleton, so that a combination of interest was contained in this generous gift.

That same evening we had a rehearsal of Sheridan's comedy of 'The Rivals,' as I had been asked to play Mrs Malaprop in the private theatricals which were to take place at Westwood House as soon as the rebuilding there should be completed. This was accomplished early in July, when we all left London and took up our abode at Sydenham, where there was to be a garden party on the 9th July, and three performances of the intended private theatricals later on. The whole transformation of the mansion and projected doings there seemed to me to be quite an Aladdin-Palace kind of celerity in achievement, but I was installed in a peaceful apartment called 'Mrs Cowden's room,' where my friends amiably placed a portrait of Shakespeare over the mantelpiece, and where I could write at perfect leisure, for I was then finishing my story of 'Uncle Peep and I,' which I had begun at the commencement of the year in compliance with a request made by Mrs Huntington that I would write a book for American children, having written so much that their elders enjoyed. By dint of working all night by gaslight, and of perpetual hammering and knocking all day, everything was ready for the garden party, which went

off brilliantly ; hosts of invited friends, a
Hungarian band on the lawn, and a part
song (sung by amateur ladies and gentlemen) especially composed for the occasion,
called 'Congratulatory Ode to commemorate
the restoration and re-opening of Westwood
House, Sydenham, on the 9th July 1881.'

The three performances of Mark Lemon's
pleasant farce, 'Domestic Economy' (in
which Mr Augustus Littleton played the
husband who stays at home to make the
pudding, and Sabilla the wife who goes out
to hoe potatoes), and Sheridan's comedy of
'The Rivals' (in which Mr Alfred Littleton
played Captain Absolute, and I Mrs Malaprop), took place on the 25th, 26th, 27th
July. The first and third of these performances were for friends, while the second
performance (by the kind thoughtfulness
of Mr . Littleton and his sons) was given
for the entertainment of the household
servants and all the workpeople who had
been employed in the restoration of Westwood House (amounting to nearly 200).

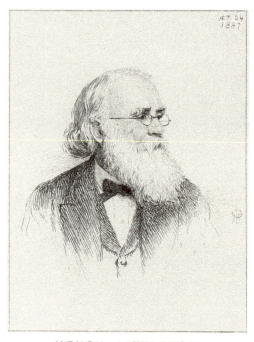

HENRY LITTLETON.

One of these workmen was heard to say
of Mrs Malaprop, 'That isn't really an old
woman ; it's a young woman *got up* old.'
I thought this a very genuine and gratifying
testimony to my being able to act well at
seventy-two years of age. I may mention,
as a characteristic trait of my liking for
preserving matters that possess a charm of
sympathetic remembrance for me, that I
then played Mrs Malaprop in the same
carefully-kept costume (made by myself
from an exquisitely painted china silk given
to me by an enthusiastic lady who heard
I was going to act in 1847), ornamented
with the same stage diamonds, and that I
used the same fan, the same pink three-
cornered note for Captain Absolute's inter-
cepted one to Lydia Languish, and the
same large letter with a huge seal for that
which Sir Anthony writes (both brought
out of Mrs Malaprop's pocket in the scene
where she causes Captain Absolute to read
from his the words, 'The old weather-
beaten she-dragon who guards you'). And

I possess the same dress, now that I am writing this at eighty-six years old. So much for innate individuality of disposition! One of the interesting visits we paid was to Sir Henry Bessemer and his lady, who invited us to dine at their charming house on Denmark Hill. He had laid out its grounds and the interior of the dwelling itself in the most artistic and scientific style imaginable. As simple-mannered as original-minded, he escorted us round himself, showing and explaining to us his many ingenious and beautiful contrivances. One of the apartments leading into a conservatory, he had both fitted up with mirrors so placed as to give what Dan Chaucer calls 'sly reflections,' and produced a curiously pleasant effect. He took me in to dinner, and conversed, in easily familiar terms, of the mode in which a tunnel is carried through a mountain, because I had asked how it was that the engineers at each end could conduct it so straightly as to meet precisely at the point needed. We took our way

back to Genova by Coblentz, Wiesbaden,
Frankfurt, Stuttgart, and Innsbruck and
the Brenner Pass, where we were favoured
by distant views of the Dolonite Peaks,
made visible to us by brilliant moonlight.

On our return home, having been asked
to contribute a paper to the 'Century
Magazine,' I wrote 'Leigh Hunt; a Descriptive Sketch,' and, to please a fancy I
had for attempting a story which should
be quite comprehensible and interesting, yet
containing not one single name, I wrote 'A
Story without a Name,' which was published
in 'The Girl's Own Paper.'

1882 began pleasantly with a visit from
our friend, Mr Littleton, who, after that,
made it an annual one for several succeeding
years, spending some weeks in this more
genial climate during the winter season. He
invited us to Westwood again, that we might
hear Gounod's grand work, 'The Redemption,' which was to be performed at the
Birmingham Festival that August. Accordingly, in June, we went to England, where we

were in good time for rehearsals of an amateur performance that was to take place in July. The entertainment consisted of Shakespeare's ' As you Like It,' in which Sabilla acted Audrey, preceded by a pro- logue which I had been asked to write and deliver myself. I made it in the form of a dialogue between Mrs Malaprop and Mrs Cowden, so that it afforded scope for num- erous Malapropisms that decidedly amused the audience.

That August, having an invitation from our dear and many-year friend, Alexander Ireland, to visit him and his family at Bowden, near Manchester, I travelled up and spent a pleasant few days there. They gave a large party of notabilities there one evening to meet me, which honour somewhat abashed my shyness, but which I felt grateful for as

On the 23d August we went to hear the rehearsal of ' The Redemption,' conducted by the glorious composer himself. At its conclusion, Gounod mustered sufficient English to address the orchestra with these kindly, courteous words :—

'Gentlemen, I could rather have believed this to have been a second performance than a first rehearsal, so correctly have you played.'

On the 25th we travelled down to Birmingham, and on the 26th we heard the first rehearsal of 'The Redemption,' previous to which we sat near to Gounod, to whom we were introduced, and he introduced to us his daughter Jeanne.

I said, '*Ah, la Dodelinette?*' and he answered, '*Oui, la Dodelinette,*' for it was to her that he had dedicated his charming lullaby thus named, and which he saw that we knew.

The next evening Gounod was invited to dine with us by Mr Littleton, and as Sabilla and I could speak French, he, much to my delight, was seated near to us.

He took me in to dinner, and he and I being next each other, I could enjoy his bright conversation to perfection. Mr

Littleton told him that he had already
made arrangement for ten different performances, at various provincial towns, for
the performance of 'The Redemption,' at
which Gounod frankly manifested his satisfaction ; and when I began to ecstacise on
the sublimity of the work, he owned that
he nearly shed tears as he wrote its concluding bars, so intensely had he felt the
delight of composing it.

When I told him how keenly I sympathised
with this feeling, and how I thought that,
upon the completion of a work into which
one has put one's heart, one feels inspired
to commence another, he said, ' *Commencer
un œuvre d'art qu'on aime, est comme un
mariage d'amour.*' And as he uttered the
words, what sparkling expression there was
in his eloquent eyes.

After dinner he accompanied his daughter
in the song, 'Loin du Pays,' by himself, and
afterwards in the song 'Souviens toi que
je t'aime' from his opera of 'Mireille.'
She sang with charming sentiment and

feeling. Just before he began accompanying her she made us laugh by saying, '*Non, papa, tu te trompes*,' because he had made some slight variation in the opening passage. The idea of telling my adored Gounod that he tripped in music seemed to me beyond measure strange and droll.

The morning when Gounod came to call upon us to take leave, he had left his hat on the table, and I, on his departing, took it to him, saying, '*Je suis faché de vous présenter votre chapeau, Mr Gounod.*' He promptly replied, '*Je crois que vous ne me mettriez pas à la porte, n'est ce pas.*'

He was altogether fascinating to me personally as well as composerly.

I met several distinguished gentlemen at that Birmingham Festival, two of whom, Professor Mahaffy and Mr Edward Broadfield, were drawn thither by the superlative treat of music we then had, and who occupied seats near to ours during its performance.

One morning I had the pleasure of hearing Mr Barnby try over the 'Sanctus'

in Gounod's just-composed MS. Mass, and
I heard that Gounod had said, in his finely
imaginative way, 'When I composed that
"Sanctus" I seemed to see the assembled mul-
titude kneeling in devout contemplation of
the holy mystery.'

From Birmingham we returned to Westwood, and thence we left for the Continent,
on the 10th September, taking our way
back by Coblentz to Munich.

After taking tickets there for the Brenner
Pass, we heard that there was talk of inter-
ruption on the railway line, and that we should
not be able to get beyond Botzen. Inundation
was hinted at, but spoken of as insignificant.

When we reached Sterzig, some gentlemen
and ladies came kindly with umbrellas, asking
us whether we would not halt there, but
hearing that the hotel was a quarter of a
mile off, and seeing there was a heavy rain
pouring down, we thought the risk of taking
severe colds seemed worse than proceeding,
so we asked the guard whether he was going on to Brixen. He said yes, but added

that telegrams had been received to say that no more accommodation of any kind was to be had there. Nevertheless, we, knowing that there were more houses at Brixen than we could see at Sterzig, resolved to 'stick to our ship,' as we told the guard, and proceed with him to Brixen.

On arrival there, Sabilla saw an omnibus waiting, and we made for it, but were told by its driver that it was engaged by some *Herrschaft*. We replied that we would ask them to permit us to share it with them, and we jumped in.

The driver, finding that his expected *Herrschaft* did not appear, drove us into Brixen, telling us he knew of a house there, kept by people who might be persuaded to let us lodge with them.

In a narrow, arcaded street he drove up to the premises of a prosperous wax-candle maker and soap-boiler, and, after a parley with the owner's family, we were taken into the house.

Passing through the curious vaulted basement, that looked like a smuggler's cave
stuffed full of casks and packing-cases, we
were conducted upstairs, where we found
large and clean rooms, bedizened, Tyrolese
fashion, with pictures and crucifixes, clocks,
toy china and an extremely curious wooden
figure, life-size, of St Carlo Borromeo, which
we were assured had been sculptured by a
blind man. The Tyrolese are very artistic,
and are especially clever in wood-sculpture.

Most fortunate we esteemed ourselves.
The people, kind as possible, giving up their
best sleeping - room to us and making us
thoroughly comfortable and at home with
them. The daughter used to fly about
with a stentorian voice and cheery face,
evidently enjoying the scrimmage, dashing
on a straw hat to fetch water from the well
or to the 'Elephant Hotel' for our meals.
Of an evening she used to clamber on to
a chair and place a light beneath a picture
of the Madonna, while often we used to
hear, before retiring for the night, the Litany

being chanted by youthful voices in a chamber above.

Of this energetic maiden her mother told us a characteristic anecdote, that, when the hospital at Brixen had been struck by lightning and burnt, her daughter had carried down some of the patients pick-a-back, which other maidens would not do, so her courage was known in all Brixen. This daughter, 'Lotte,' gave us sad news of cottages washed away, fields destroyed, etc., and the cruel rain continued to carry sorrow and desolation with it. At the post-office were stacks of post parcels awaiting possibility of transit, while the letters were carried on men's backs over the high mountains, and the poor fellows were working day and night.

An odd, old-world custom was still retained in Brixen, which is represented in Mendelssohn's opera 'Son and Stranger,' as well as in Wagner's 'Meistersänger,' and which had a curiously-mingled effect of implied peril and assurance of protection from danger. A watchman with his dog passed the house where we were staying, every hour between ten p.m. and three o'clock a.m., announcing the hour and exhorting to prayer in a quaint call. This—while the inundations went on, and the dull, continuous downpour of rain accompanied the sound of the watchman's voice—was most impressive, but when the weather somewhat cleared, I used to listen to the hourly announcement and exhortation with revived hope and trust. The walks we were then able to take were very interesting, and on the whole our enforced month's stay at Brixen had been productive of good. The pure fresh air, its kindly people, its interesting cathedral and environs, had improved our health and gratified our taste. The hospitable Kirschbaumers were kindly courteous to the very last moment, coming up to the station with us, seeing us off with tears in their eyes. Finding that return, by the remainder of the Brenner Pass, to Italy was still impracticable, we retraced our way, and went back through Munich, Carlsruhe, and round by the Mont Cenis Pass to Genoa.

In the autumn of that year an enormously large comet was visible from our house here. I got up several times at four o'clock in the morning to see it thoroughly. It extended along the eastern quarter of the heavens, fiery-red and portentous in magnitude, making one think of Milton's words,—'Like a comet burn'd, that fires the length of Ophiuchus huge in the arctic sky.'

The next year, 1883, I was asked to contribute to the 'St Nicholas Magazine,' a periodical for children, and I sent for insertion my juvenile drama called 'Puck's Pranks ; ' and Mrs Meynell requesting me to send her a paper on ancient cookery for the magazine she was editing ('Merry England'), I wrote 'On English Cookery in Shakespeare's Time,' that she much approved.

In the summer Sabilla and I took our usual change to cooler and inland air. We made our first acquaintance with Baden-Baden, which we subsequently frequently visited. From Baden-Baden, that summer, we went to our pleasant Rhenish quarters at Coblentz, remaining there some weeks, and returning home to Genoa. There, in the winter, we had a series of admirable lectures on English literature, delivered by Mr James Cappon, a most welcome and exceptional treat in Genoa. He paid us several visits at our house here, and we found him as excellent in conversation as in lecturing.

We made a novel experience in 1884 by going through the St Gothard Tunnel into Germany, and were enchanted by the scenery we passed through, and much pleased with the capital arrangements of the railway line all along. We made a longish stay at Carlsruhe, seeing it properly for the first time. Its mixture of ducal court refinement, with the simplicity of a country town, impressed me so fascinatingly that I wrote four sonnets, comparing it with my favourite Enfield and Dulwich for peculiar charm.

When 1885 began, and Mr Littleton as usual came to see us in January, he invited us to go and visit him and Mrs Littleton in the summer, and go with them to hear Gounod's 'Mors et Vita' at the Birmingham Festival in August. There was also to be an amateur performaace at Westwood of Ross Neil's charming play of 'The King and the Angel,' its subject being the one given in prose by Leigh Hunt, called 'King Robert of Sicily,' in verse by Long-fellow under the same title, and by William Morris, entitled 'The Proud King.' So tempting a proposal was, of course, accepted by Sabilla and me; and on the 18th July the promised performance took place most brilliantly. I found that Ross Neil has introduced a beautifully dramatic and true-to-nature incident, by making a woman one of the means of effecting the transformed king's reform. She is a princess, betrothed to the king, treated by him, during his

haughty, overbearing first self, with neglect
and indifference, but who, by gentle and
tenderly considerate behaviour to him in
his period of transformation to a wretched
outcast, aids in awakening him to a sense
of his previous misconduct. The Birmingham Festival's first introduction to the
public of Gounod's grandly devout ' Mors
et Vita' was an immense treat to me,
though I sadly missed the presence of its
great composer, who was unable to come
over to England. I tried to content myself with thinking of all he had said and
looked when I had met him during the
performance of 'The Redemption,' three
years before. During this return to Birmingham I was taken by my dear, kind,
long-esteemed friend, Mr Sam Timmins, to
see the Shakespeare Library, and it was
pleasant to me to see almost every other
person that passed touch his hat to him
as we walked there together. The building
for the library was noble in itself, but the
collection of treasures within was magnifi-

cent, and the order preserved—both in
the accommodation of readers and in
the arrangement of books—was perfectly
admirable. Of course, the room especially
dedicated to the Shakespeare Library was
the chief point of interest to my guide and
to me, and he had one of the curators,
with the keys of the bookcases, to open
for my inspection some of the rarest and
choicest volumes preserved there. Then
he took me into the chief reading-room,
where there was a bust of himself, and
told me of George Dawson (who for some
time was believed to have been the originator of the idea of this library) having
delivered a speech on the very spot where
we stood, to the effect that it was Mr
Timmins who, in reality, was the first to
originate the idea, and to promote its ful-
filment. As I sat there, Mr Timmins
reading to me, in a low voice, an extract
from this identical speech, eloquent and
fervent in the extreme, I was deeply
touched, and the reader himself was full

P

of emotion. The whole visit was peculiarly interesting, and both Mr Timmins and I congratulated ourselves on having thus been able to achieve it, having looked forward to it for some years. I showed him the miniature ring I wear, telling him I had brought his friend, C. C.-C. (my other self), to be with me in this noble Shakespeare Library; and Mr Timmins feelingly alluded to the times when my beloved came to lecture in Birmingham, and when their first interview took place as referred to in the two sonnets I addressed to our constant friend. On leaving, I was taken to a large book kept for the purpose of registering visitors, and he asked me to sign my name therein, which signature I found, to my great gratification, came next to that of no less a personage than Russell Lowell. I may here be permitted to mention that I have ever felt grateful for the liberal way in which distinguished Shakespearians have treated me with a cordial *fraternity* as one of their brotherhood. In America, as well as England, this has been the case. Even now, as I write, comes a letter from Mr Timmins, dated February 22d, 1896, giving me an account of the intended celebration of Shakespeare's birthday on the 23d of April. As long ago as when the Reverend N. J. Halpin wrote his 'Dramatic Unities of Shakespeare,' published in 1849, he sent me his book and corresponded with me; Dr Ingleby did the same, and nowadays Frederick Haines, one of the trustees of the Shakespeare birthplace, at Stratford-on-Avon, writes me delightful letters, while Richard Savage, its librarian, sends me dried flowers from the garden there. From America I have received such continued courtesies and kindnesses that I have felt as if we had, in Shakespeare's words, ' shook hands as over a vast, and embraced, as it were, from the ends of opposed winds.' Dr Horace Howard Furness sends me each volume of his magnificent ' Variorum Edition of Shakespeare ' as it is

successively published; Dr W. J. Rolfe
has sent me his 'Friendly Edition of
Shakespeare' with generous hand, calling
me its godmother because I gave it that
name; Professor Hiram Corson has presented me with the books he has written
on that and other poetical subjects, besides
paying me a visit here when he came to
Europe; and Mr George H. Calvert sent
me his 'Shakespeare; a Biographic and
Æsthetic Study,' and also several works he
wrote on various themes. From charming
Celia Thaxter we had a visit one Christmas,
when she gaily helped us stone raisins,
etc., for our Christmas pudding, and told us
ghost-stories, and proved herself the exact
being that dear Mr James T. Fields de-
scribes her in one of the many delightful
letters he wrote, telling me that he always
called her 'the laughing girl,' and when
he sent me her poetical prose book,
'Among the Isles of Shoals.' On taking
leave of us that Christmas she gave me a
dainty volume of her 'Poems,' many

pages of which she adorned by sketches,
in natural colours, of flowers, weeds, etc.,
dashed across the page. Mrs James Fields
we likewise saw more than once on
occasions when she was in Europe. Her
books of poems, 'Under the Olives,' and
her 'Singing Shepherd,' were her kind
gifts to me. Miss Sarah Orme Jewett, her
attached friend, always accompanied her
when she came to see us, and from her I
have received several of her vivid literary-
pictures of American life. Similar ameni-
ties of correspondence and presents of her
clever works I have had from Miss Imogen
Guiney ; so that from American ladies—
and several others unmentioned here—I
have received abundant and memorable
tokens of friendly feeling. In the November of that year I began writing my
'Shakespeare's Self, as revealed in his
Writings,' and it was printed in the
American Magazine, 'Shakespeariana,' for
April 1886.

One of the performances of Wagner's

'Parsifal' at Bayreuth being announced to take place in the last-named year, Sabilla and I resolved we would go thither. Arrangements having been made with the authorities, who appointed quarters for the accommodation of the numerous visitors thronging thither, we were so fortunate as to have had selected for us apartments in the house of a particularly hospitable couple, with whom we soon felt quite at home, so kindly attentive were they to our every comfort and convenience. The town being at some distance from the theatre, we engaged a small carriage, belonging to our hosts, for the whole of our stay at Bayreuth. The performances were arranged with excellent care and forethought ; between each act trumpets sounded the call from the opera of 'Lohengrin,' and the audience were able to enjoy a refection at the Restauration outside the theatre, no one but those who had been present there being allowed to take seats at each meal. The music was admirably given ; the players in the orchestra, stationed out of sight, took their places, *ready-tuned ;* and the vocal artists were all excellent. Besides ' Parsifal,' the ' Tristan and Isolde ' was performed ; but I must own that I was so much affected by a sense of weariness, after listening to ' Parsifal ' and subsequently to the first act of ' Tristan and Isolde,' that I presented my ticket to our obliging hostess, who was an enthusiastic Wagnerite. I am a warm admirer of Wagner in his poetical treatment of ' Der fliegende Holländer ' and ' Tannhäuser,' the first of which the composer has been said to denounce as ' too melodious,' but which I find beautifully and appropriately weird ; while the imaginative charm he has imparted throughout the Venus-haunted knight's career in ' Tannhäuser ' is, to me, completely bewitching.

From Bayreuth we took flight to our ' Delightful Dresden,' which we found attractive as ever, though we deeply regretted the loss of our admirable actor, Dettmer, and of the as admirable baritone, Degele, who had both died in the interim. However, very soon after our revisits to the Hoftheater, we learned to appreciate the versatile talent of an actor named Klein, who impersonated, with equal verity, *President la Roquette* (a real man living in Louis XIV.'s time, and said to have been the prototype of Molière's 'Tartuffe'); the cruel and implacable Duke of Alva; a lively Spanish page; a self-made rich merchant, with white hair; and a middle-aged major, still youthful enough in manner to be irresistible to young ladies. In all and each of these characters Klein was wonderfully true to nature.

One evening after our arrival, while we were seated in our usual places in the stalls, a pencilled note was brought to us by the stall-keeper, on which was written : 'Look up to the box on the right of the royal one, and you will see some friends who love you.' They proved to be the three ladies Huntington, whom we had known before in Dresden in 1880 ; and when we met on the grand staircase, after the performance, they spoke most earnestly and affectionately to us. Our stay in Dresden was as entirely agreeable as our visits there had always been on previous occasions ; and we returned to Genoa by Zurich and the St Gothard Pass.

The editor of ' The Girl's Own Paper ' having requested me to send him a contribution, I wrote ' Shakespeare as the Girl's Friend,' which was printed in the number for 4th June 1887. Later on, my ' Story Without a Name,' and my ' Benemilda ; or the Path of Duty,' also appeared in that graceful periodical. Inviting our niece Valeria to accompany us that summer, we went to Brunnen, and took up our abode in the Waldstätterhof, on the shore of the lake of the four cantons, surrounded by the glorious mountain snow peaks. Amid that sublime scenery I wrote my ' Centennial Biographic Sketch of Charles Cowden-Clarke.' This, and my ' Memorial Sonnets,' etc., kind Mr Littleton caused to be printed in order that I might have copies to give to friends.

From Brunnen we proceeded to Baden-Baden, where we much enjoyed our time,

for we were so fortunate as to make acquaintance with several musically and generally-
accomplished families, who became lasting
friends of ours whenever we subsequently
revisited Baden-Baden's delicious greenwood
shades.

In my opinion, it is extremely pleasant to
see how the young ladies come in from the
kitchen, where they have been engaged in
household superintendence, and in acquiring
practical experience, still wearing their neat
little white aprons with bibs, and then seat
themselves at the pianoforte to take part, with
one of their parents, in some duet by a
favourite composer. It seems to me that this
wise combination of domesticity and skill in
music forms a perfect feminine education, as
wise as it is productive of pleasure. And it
was our gratification to witness more than one
instance of this judicious bringing up young
ladies, rendering them able to become
thoroughly competent mistresses of a house
when they marry, as well as artistically accomplished companions to their husbands.

In our summer journey, the following year,
we were accompanied by our niece Porzia,
whom we invited to enjoy the cooler air of
Tyrol and Germany. Very soon after our
arrival at Innsbrück, Sabilla made the welcome discovery that a peasant play was to be
given at the Sommertheater not far off, in the
afternoon, so we all three drove there, and
found a small neat theatre, built of boards, in
a Restauration Garten, and where we took
our tickets for the best places (like the stalls)
at a franc each. All the performers were
amateurs, mostly peasants, and the first actress
the wife of a shoemaker! She was perfectly
charming; and the rest were more than re-
spectable. The piece was of the high romantic style, and consisted of a mediæval
story pertaining to a certain castle near to
Innsbrück. It was called ' The Tournament
of Kronstein,' and most of the characters
figured in antique armour, while the widow-
countess-heroine wore picturesque mediæval
costumes. She looked like an old-master
portrait, was refined in her voice, her look,

her movements, and was altogether thoroughly unconventional and interesting.

One day, opposite to us at *table d'hôte*, we saw two ladies take their seats very quietly, one of them wearing a simple white frock, and looking so girlish, that Sabilla whispered to me,—' Though that young lady looks so unpretending and quiet, she seems to me to be accustomed to be "a somebody."' On speaking to her after dinner, we found that she was no other than the superlative pianiste, Fanny Davies, and she said, ' I had already recognised you, for you had been pointed out to me at the Birmingham Festival as Vincent Novello's daughters.' She became delightfully familiar and friendly with us, and generously offered to play to us. The obliging master of the hotel lent us his own parlour, which had a better pianoforte in it than the one in the readingroom ; and many an evening's superb treat of music by the best composers did Fanny Davies give us. Ever after, she has been

called by me 'my Charmer'; and numerous
have been the charming feasts she has
given us, when meeting her in Germany, or
when she favoured us by visits to us here
in Genoa. From Innsbrück we went to
Munich, where Sabilla and Porzia were
much interested to hear the early opera
of Wagner's called 'Die Feen,' which was
got up with the usual poetry and beauty that
distinguish the performances at the Munich
Hoftheater.

We left Munich for Stuttgart, where we
daily used to listen to the fine military band
on the Platz, and to the chorale that was
each noon to be '*blasen*' from the tower of
the *Stifts Kirche*, a curious antique cere-
monial observed there. It was most interesting to hear this old chorale blown by
instruments sounding like a gigantic Æolian
harp up there, among the angles of architectural ornamentation belonging to the
quaint old church.

One evening a Generalissimo having arrived, a serenade was given to him, which

I enjoyed throughout. At eight o'clock the sound of a military band became audible, and soon came moving on in double file, a long array of soldiers bearing coloured lanterns and playing a bright march. Then they drew up at the angle of the two streets on which our hotel abutted, and began with an appealing *fanfare* of trumpets. Then followed two grave pieces—like chorales—sounding forth majestically and full-toned. Then followed a quick, brisk movement, upon which the entire vast crowd burst forth with loud and enthusiastic '*Hochs*'; while the Generalissimo presented himself at the window and saluted the crowd. The whole thing was a sight and sound never to be forgotten, and I thought myself fortunate to have had so many opportunities of enjoying German summers and delightful Italian home-winter-residence, enhanced by English comforts and dear, ever-loved English ties.

We made some stay at Carlsruhe on our return journey, and were charmed with that

delightful lyric artist, Mailhae, who acts as
finely as she sings. As Reiza, in Weber's
opera of 'Oberon,' she was exquisite, especially in the last aria, so descriptive of
utter grief and despair, she was content
to remain perfectly motionless, with one
arm drooping at her side, and the other
listlessly lying across her person, while her
head inclined gently down, giving completely
the effect of complete woe-begone sense of
loss. In other characters she is quite as
dramatically natural. As Catherine the Shrew
(in Gotz's opera taken from Shakespeare's
'Taming of the Shrew') she was admirable ; and in the gay little Tyrolese afterpiece she enacted a rustic maiden, making
her easy, active, playful and pouting all in
turn, with bewitching effect.

The year 1889 opened brilliantly for us.
Miss Fanny Davies and Miss Grist paid us
a flying visit here in Genoa, when 'my
Charmer' played us, in her wonted generous
and perfect style, Mendelssohn, Chopin,
Rubinstein, etc., and in the evening the

ladies enjoyed a performance at the *Marionette* Theatre, to which Sabilla invited them as an Italian curiosity of entertainment. We made a change in our summer excursion that year, thinking we would try if a less distant one might prove equally effectual as a refuge from too perpetual residence by the seaside. Accordingly, we went to a beautiful spot on the north side of one of the Turinese Hills, called San Genesio. Magnificent view towards the Val d'Aosta, finely-wooded environment, and a spacious, well-built hotel promised well. Delicious wanderings in the woods, with occasional luxurious rests on commodiously-placed seats under the trees, made our days pass pleasantly, and during our stay I had the exceptional delight of seeing many a sunrise, besides beholding an eclipse of the moon from its commencement to its close. A rural touch about some of the ways of the house brought us acquainted with a flight of pigeons, three of them being special friends of ours. They used to come as regularly as possible for crumbs from our hands; and once, when Sabilla and I had taken refuge in a shady reading-room, where its half-closed shutters and open door made the excessive heat bearable while she was playing on the pianoforte for me, in trotted our three feathered friends, evidently come to seek for us.

However, notwithstanding the many attractions of San Genesio, we agreed that, being in Italy, it did not afford sufficiently cool air for our summer need, so we went straight to Lucerne, where we found remarkable contrast from our just-left sojourn at San Genesio to this Swiss resort, with its more than a thousand feet above the sea coolness and its crowded hotel. During our stay there, whom should we see arrive but Mr Alfred Littleton and Dr Dulcken—the former, as always, full of amiable courtesy and attention to me, the latter, one of the best of conversers, who generally took his seat beside mine, and

Q

gave me what Dr Johnson calls 'good talk.'

Some time afterwards a gentleman darted out of a room on the opposite side of the corridor to ours and said, 'I think one of you ladies is Mrs Cowden - Clarke.' Sabilla pointed to me, whereupon he began, 'I want to speak a word with you,' and then proceeded to tell me that he was Mr Armstrong, that his father was the American publisher who wished to bring out a new and complete edition of my 'Girlhood of Shakespeare's Heroines.' This project was, to my great joy, ultimately carried out, and more than forty years after the first edition had been printed in London, this new and complete one was simultaneously published by Messrs Armstrong of New York, and Messrs Hutchinson of Paternoster Square, London. I may here take occasion to say that all my experience of publishers has been most agreeable. Contrary to the prejudiced opinion sometimes expressed, that authors

and publishers are often antagonistic in
their transactions, I have invariably met
with courtesy and kindliness. Ever since
an interview I once had with Lord Byron's
John Murray, another that I had with
Mr Colburn, I have been treated with consideration, and even with amiability. I
cannot forget, for instance, that when I
wrote to Messrs Longman & Company, requesting them to give me a particular
article I wanted from an expensive book
they were bringing out, saying that I
could not then afford to purchase the whole
work, and mentioning that my father had
in former years taught Miss Longman to
play the organ, the reply I received was
not only couched in most obliging terms,
but was accompanied by the gift I had
requested.

I may also mention the behaviour of
Messrs Manning & Mason when they
had printed my ' Concordance to Shakespeare,'
and I went to their establishment in Ivy
Lane in order to sign my name to each

copy, all was prepared for me with utmost regard to my convenience during the long day I spent there from early morning to late evening, listening to each hour that boomed from the bell of St Paul's cathedral. I must not omit to record that from American publishers I have likewise received tokens of marked regard. Messrs Munroe, Messrs Roberts of Boston, Mr J. P. Putnam, and Messrs Appleton of New York, have each and all shown me much that proves the courtesy of publishers to authors. My dear Mr James Fields was noted for his goodness to authors, and to him I not only am indebted for numerous delightful letters, but also for treasured gifts of his own poems and essays, his charming 'Yesterdays with Authors' and his 'Letter to Leigh Hunt in Elysium,' written in a style remarkably akin to the playful spirit of Leigh Hunt's own manner.

From Lucerne we went to Lugano and stayed at the Hôtel du Parc, which I re-membered had been so rapturously described

by a gentleman whom my Charles and I
had met at Arona as long ago as 1862,
that I had often longed to visit this
particular hostelry. It proved a realisa-
tion of my wish ; being a monastery con-
verted into a hotel, and containing fine
long corridors with plenteous side-rooms.
Moreover, the apartment appointed for
Sabilla's and my reception overlooked a
garden in which there was a Moresco
alcove, where an excellent band played,
morning and evening, a capital selection
of music. On the evening of our first
arrival at Lugano, this band breathed out
its enchanting sounds, while a soft moonlight gave perfection to this combination
of beauty. Deeply grateful did I feel
for having had so many of my dearest and
highest ideals vouchsafed to me during my
long and exceptionally blest life. The
whole of our stay in Lugano was most
pleasant to us, and we did not return to
Genoa until the end of September.

At Easter, in the following year, we had

another melodious flying visit from 'my Charmer,' Fanny Davies, but when the summer came we ourselves flew from Italian heat to seek change into cooler inland air; and having so much enjoyed our autumnal experience at Lugano, we thought we would try whether we could find freshness there. Our reception was pleasant, the same congenial apartment overlooking the garden, but, alas! no band in the Moresco alcove, the season not being the one when the players resorted there. However, we were not without music, for a nightingale saluted us on arrival, carolling in 'full-throated ease' among the trees of the hotel garden, one end of which overlooks the lake. As a farther regale to our music-loving ears, one day, as we were pacing up and down one of the long corridors, we heard the sounds of a pianoforte, and, on inquiry, learned that it was the daughter of the house practising. The playing was so good, and the pieces played so excellent, that we asked whether it would be considered

indiscreet were we to beg admission to listen.
The reply from the mother of the young
lady was most courteous, and when we
knocked at the door of the room next day,
we were received with fascinating sweetness
of manner, and were played to for at least
an hour, with charming liberality, pieces by
Chopin, Schumann, etc., etc. We were indulged with several of these artistic treats
by this accomplished young lady player,
who was as simple-mannered and girlish-
gay as she was skilled in music ; for when
Sabilla gave her a copy of her 'Bluebeard'
books, she skipped about the room with
joy. English, as well as French and Italian,
were known to her, besides German, so that
she could enjoy the perusal perfectly. We,
of course, took some drives along the finely-
kept, steep roads around Lugano, but notwithstanding its many attractions, its perse-
vering heat made us feel that we should
do well to remove into higher and cooler
air ; therefore, we took leave of the obliging
proprietors of the Hôtel du Parc and their

charming daughter with heartiest feelings of gratitude. The courtesy of the proprietor took final climax in the mode wherewith he arranged our departure, for we found awaiting us at the door his own carriage and pair to convey us to the station, while he himself issued from his cloistral court-yard and presented us a choice bouquet each from his daughter with her best re-membrances. He was interested when he found we were going to Baden-Baden, as he himself was a native of that place, and he stood for some minutes telling us of the Grand Duke and Duchess of Baden, and of the Duchess of Mechlinburg-Strelitz, who had given him a diamond ring which he showed us, and said how gracious they had been to him when they stayed at his hotel. In thanking him for all his courtesies to us, we told him that it seemed as if he took us for some of these royalties, he treated us so distinguishedly. We halted for a night in the St Gothard Hotel at Lucerne, obtaining from the window of

our room a fine view of the chief portion
of the town on the opposite side of the
lake, while the lake itself was crowned by
heights as far as the Rigi Culm, forming
a noble panorama. It was illumined by
myriads of lights—electric ones, gas ones,
red and green ones—giving the effect of a
superb and extensive illumination, while near
at hand were the lights of the railway
station and its illuminated clock. These
brilliancies gave sufficient light in our room
to enable us to dispense with candles when
we went to bed—a dispensation that always
pleases me. Next morning, at dawn, I still
enjoyed the spacious prospect, though under
very different aspect. Without getting up
from my bed I could see Lucerne and its
two spires, in a grey veil of mist, looking
very like that wonderful picture by Cuyp,
'A View of Dort,' which I once saw at
the Exhibition of Old Masters in London.
Then, at sunrise, my scene was lighted up
brilliantly, and lasted thus for a short
interval, till, later on, though the sky

clouded over, it still afforded me an exquisite picture.

On arriving at Baden-Baden, we almost
immediately found our health and spirits
improve from the change to the green at-
mosphere that has always seemed to me to
distinguish that picturesque spot. Its early
hours, its orderly way of providing for the
comfort and convenience of visitors, its
artistic resources, its friendly hospitalities
combine to make it a specially healthful as
well as agreeable sojourn to us, and I owe
it most grateful regard. On arrival, we
heard that Don Pedro, the Emperor of
Brazil, was again there. We had had
gracious notice from him when he had
been in Baden-Baden at the time our niece
Valeria was with us in 1887, and His Im-
perial Highness was as gracious as ever
towards us, while our curtseys were deeper
than ever, since in the interim he had lost
his throne. One day we had the opportunity of hearing a discourse from the
celebrated religious reformer, Père Hya-

cinthe, in the English Church at Baden-
Baden. His discourse was chiefly concern-
ing his ardent desire to see peace and
goodwill and mutual forbearance between
all churches and forms of religious worship.
His manner was earnest, and, at the beginning, tranquil, but rose into vehemence
and urgency as he proceeded. His French
was, of course, perfect, his enunciation was
clear, his voice effective. He was very
eloquent, inasmuch as he was never for a
moment at a loss for pertinent expressions
and telling phrases. He had a way of
lapsing occasionally into quite familiar
manner and utterance, then rising into more
emphatic and florid appeal. He dwelt with
hearty congratulation on the present possibility of *speaking out freely* on matters of
belief and form of worship, in contrast with
the former suppression of opinion and op-
pression of liberal ideas. We had resolved
to walk back, so we strolled leisurely along
the ever-lovely Lichtenthaler Allee, till
we reached the milk establishment where

the cows assemble at five o'clock in the afternoon, affording delicious drink to dozens of children and invalids. The extreme heat made a frothed-up tankard of the lily-white beverage very welcome to us. As the water of the spring near to us had a bitter taste, and we were still thirsty that evening, which was overpoweringly hot, our ever-willing maid, Pasquina, ran out to fetch us some from a picturesque fount near the Trinkhalle, that water being famed for its purity. The fitting-up of this pretty little spring is most tasteful. It issues from a rock overgrown with green climbers, amid which a tube, in the form of a serpent (the emblem of health), seems to be sliding down the rock, and affords a perpetually gushing stream of this clear spring water.

There was an organ performance on the 6th September, which seemed so appropriate in date for celebration of the anniversary of our dear father's birthday, that Sabilla and I went to hear it in the Protestant church, where the performance took place. What

a glorious instrument is the organ, and how
tenderly is it associated in my thought. We
renewed acquaintance with a delightful composer and amiable old gentleman—Herr
Rosenhain ; and he invited us to his weekly
matinees whenever we felt inclined to drive
out to his villa at Lichtenthal. We naturally
availed ourselves of this invitation very often ;
but when we said we hoped we should not
be indiscreet in doing so, he replied, 'I
cannot see too much of those I like, or too
little of those I dislike.' On one of these
occasions, when we arrived at Villa Rosenhain, and had carriaged thither Fanny Davies
and Miss Grist, we found that there was
a rehearsal going on in the music-room, so
that we were requested to take seats in the
hall until the rehearsal was over. While we
stayed there, who should come in but Clara
Schumann (who had just arrived in Baden-
Baden), and she remained also quietly in the
hall, *whispering* to us, and leaving her hand
in mine as she talked cordially to me. I
remember feeling curiously thrilled as I

stood clasping the hand that had been dear
to Robert Schumann, and had so ably inter-
preted his compositions.　When we entered
the music-room we had the treat of hearing
Herr Rosenhain's concerto, arranged for
two pianofortes, played by himself and Fanny
Davies in admirable style; then followed
some of Schumann's songs, sung by an
amateur gentleman with a charming tenor
voice, and in a style so refined, so distinct
an enunciation of words, so touching in expression that we complimented him afterwards.　He took our praises with evident
gratification, but said that he owned to being
rather nervous while singing the Schumann
songs, as he did not feel quite sure whether
Madame Schumann might approve the *manner*
in which he sang them.　Herr Rosenhain had
a very agreeable mode of introducing certain
of his guests to each other; and among others
that morning he presented to Sabilla a gentleman who remembered being at the Bonn
Festival when she sang there, and recollected
Spohr there, as well as the incident of Lizst's

lending his gilt chairs for our Queen and Prince Albert, when they unexpectedly arrived there, as Lizst always travelled with his own splendid furniture. That same morning Herr Rosenhain introduced us to an extremely interesting personage—a sweet-faced, sweet-mannered young lady, who smiled and curtseyed to us—no other than charming Cecile Mendelssohn, grand-daughter of Felix, and namesake of his pretty wife. She became one of the most delightfully constant friends we made in Baden-Baden, and felt an immediate interest in our having known her illustrious grandfather when he was just about the age of her own when we met her. She has since married, and still retains her renowned name, as she wedded her cousin, Herr Otto Mendelssohn Bartholdy.

Altogether our stay in Baden-Baden that year was one of the most productive of enjoyment we ever had there. 1891 being the year appointed for another Mozart Musikfest in Salzburg, we resolved to go thither again that summer. The effect of his own superb Requiem being performed in the cathedral where he had so often worshipped, was to me ineffably imposing. The fine Viennese orchestra and several famed artistes played and sang, accompanied by the organ, while, as I listened, I beheld a brilliant ray of sunlight stream through the stained-glass window opposite to me, seeming as though the spirit of the divinely-inspired composer himself were present. From Salzburg we went up to 'Delightful Dresden,' as it had been a long promise to our niece Valeria that we would take her there some day ; and she and her brother Giovanni, whom we also invited, were with us during our very pleasant sojourn on this occasion. We made it our rule, as before, to enjoy every performance at the Hoftheater, where a really fine actor, named *Drach*, inspired us with ardent admiration. He impersonated Hamlet and other Shakespearian characters with true poetic and artistic inspiration. His Coriolanus, for instance, in which I could well remember Macready, appeared

to me to be worthy of all praise. Our
later years have passed placidly in alternate
summer visits to Germany and enjoyment
of home music with home pursuits, literary
or social. Speaking of literary pursuits, I
may mention that much of my reading,
latterly, has been peering into favourite old
books, with sparing perusal of modern ones ;
and I refer to the fact of my retaining the
conscientiousness that was encouraged in me
by my dear mother while I was a child, for
the sake of showing how in old age the same
characteristic exists. A volume of farces,
which has its table of contents marked by
her with a pencilled cross against those pieces
she forbade me to read, has caused me never
to peruse those particular farces. Coarseness
has ever been my abhorrence ; for well does
Shelley say in his noble 'Defence of
Poetry,'—'Obscenity is blasphemy against
the divine beauty in life ;' and Sir John
Lubbock, in his charming book, 'The
Pleasures of Life,' says,—'The soul is dyed
by its thoughts ; we cannot keep our minds

R

pure if we allow them to be sullied by detailed accounts of crime and sin.'

Therefore, I allow myself to revel in my beloved poets, and some very favourite novels, etc., on my shelves, thinking I may as well indulge my now less-strong eyesight with looking only into preferred books, especially if they have the advantage of being printed in clearly legible type.

My sister Sabilla laughingly says I might have taken for the motto of this book the words on the sun-dial in front of our Italian dwelling here, Englished thus :—'I denote only the hours of sunshine.' But I am thankful for the 'rose-coloured spectacles' I am said to wear, and I cannot do better than conclude with lines that truly show my

OLD AGE PHILOSOPHY.

In lieu of vain regret for days long flown,
I'm thankful for the joys that I have known :
When conscious that I now see less, hear less,
And walk less well, I think of happiness

Bestowed on me in fullest, dearest measure,
And hug to inmost heart the God-sent treasure.
    Oh, Memory ! that still is granted me—
For dearest, truest blisses, ecstasy
Of love and intellectual discourse,
For faculties alert and body's force ;
For power to enjoy Life's choicest gifts ;
For energy to ponder theme that lifts
The soul in lofty speculation on
High mysteries that youth delights to con,
But Age has learnt with calmness to accept
Unquestioned, as beyond our ken inept ;
For readiness of pen, that then expressed
With ease the thoughts that yearned to be
    confessed
In words ; for sympathy desired, and found
As soon as wished, from one whose wisdom
    sound
And tender eagerness to lend his aid
Were ever generously, promptly laid
At my behoof. Though years have now
    bereft
Me of these blessings manifold, those left
I'm deeply grateful for ; and more than all,
For memories that former joys recall,
Dear memories, on which I dwell and live,
Renew my sense of youth, relume, revive
My inner fire of heart, my warmth of trust,
My feeling that our Heavenly Father must

Be bounteous and benign, as He hath shown
Himself to be to me and to my own
Belovèd one, who made me happy wife
Throughout our earthly perfect married life.

THE END

Colston & Coy. Limited, Printers, Edinburgh.

For EU product safety concerns, contact us at Calle de José Abascal, 56–1°,
28003 Madrid, Spain or eugpsr@cambridge.org.